MAN *with* A HAMMER

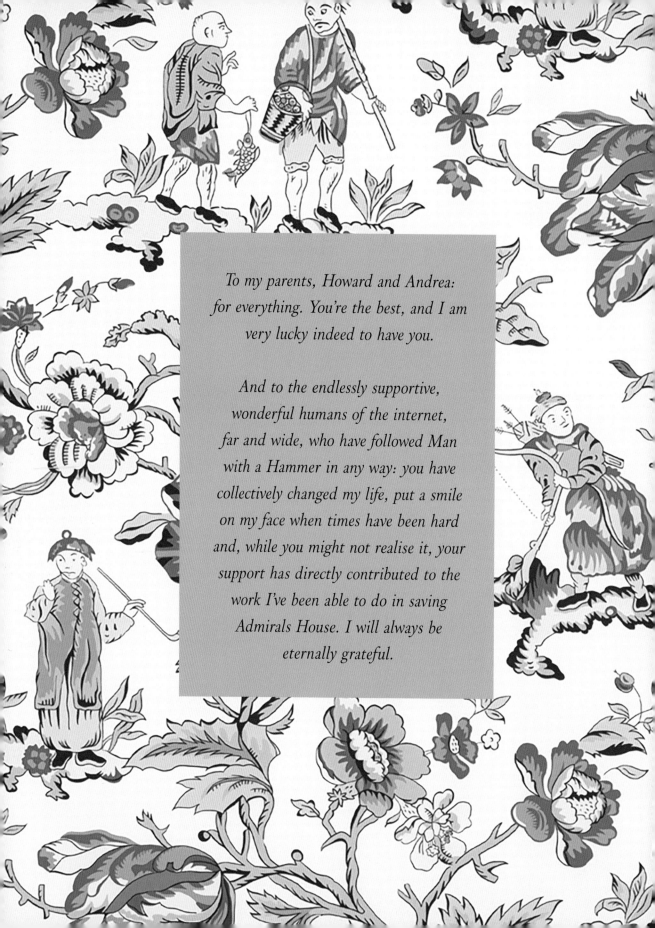

To my parents, Howard and Andrea: for everything. You're the best, and I am very lucky indeed to have you.

And to the endlessly supportive, wonderful humans of the internet, far and wide, who have followed Man with a Hammer in any way: you have collectively changed my life, put a smile on my face when times have been hard and, while you might not realise it, your support has directly contributed to the work I've been able to do in saving Admirals House. I will always be eternally grateful.

MAN *with* A HAMMER

FROM FORGOTTEN WRECK TO FOREVER
HOME – AN INSPIRING DIY TRANSFORMATION

GREG PENN

PHOTOGRAPHY BY
ANDREW BURTON

HODDER &
STOUGHTON

Room
by Room

44

The
Ground Floor

50

The
First Floor

118

The
Second Floor

156

Contents

INTRODUCTION

Renovating this old girl has easily been the hardest thing I've ever done, but also by far the most rewarding ...

Once upon a time (about four and a half years ago at the point of writing, to be precise), in a land far, far away (Devon, which to a Yorkshireman might as well be another planet), yours truly made the deeply inadvisable decision to buy, for an alarmingly bargainous price, a thirty-room, five-storey ex-naval Georgian wreck of a house by the sea. It was three times bigger than anything I'd been looking for and nearly twice the price, but it was love at first sight.

In this book I'll let you in on what the last few years have entailed, a little about the house itself and the naval hospital it would have once been a part of, a glimpse into what renovating an old lump like this with limited budget (not to mention limited skills, talent or taste) entails, and lots more besides. It's certainly not designed to be instructional (I'm learning - and often making it up - as I go along, after all), but I hope it's interesting to those of you thinking of taking on a home renovation project of your own, regardless of its size and age.

Renovating this old girl has easily been the hardest thing I've ever done, but also by far the most rewarding, and if you go into it with your eyes open, renovating is something I'd heartily recommend - with a few caveats!

But, before I get going with the dust, dirt, injuries, adventures and general shenanigans that go hand in hand with any renovation, let alone one of this magnitude, I want to tell you a bit about how all this came about.

My STORY

It would be fair to say that renovating probably wasn't a natural talent of mine ...

I was born in 1984, to (lovely) parents who would be accurately described as serial renovators. I grew up living in renovations (indeed, I've still got the tiniest of indentations in my forehead where, as a nipper, I went headfirst into some rubble) and, for a while, I just assumed that was normal. Both my folks worked full-time around trying to do the work, alongside raising two kids, so you might assume that's what gave me the bug and that getting into this sort of thing was inevitable. Well, that couldn't be further from the truth ... at least not at first.

Up until the age of thirty-ish, I'd shown no interest at all in such things. Primarily because I never thought I'd have enough cash to buy a house, as I was far too busy having a lovely time, living within my means – just – with not a lot to show for it at the end of the month. I worked in marketing on an organic farm in Northallerton, North Yorkshire, and was affectionately known very much as the office wally, incapable of doing anything remotely practical. There are enough embarrassing tales to fill the rest of this book of me being broadly useless in the eyes of a very capable farmer who could seemingly fix anything, from pole barns to complex farming equipment, with naught more than a hammer and some baler twine. While I'm a big lump and came in useful for lifting heavy stuff, for anything else I was politely asked to stay well clear.

Eventually, I was in a position to buy my first home. I'd spent most of my life in York at the time and my modest budget might have bought a shed at the bottom of someone's garden there, so that ruled that location out. My new place needed to be commutable to Northallerton, not too quiet (I'd been living in a damp cottage with no central heating in a tiny hamlet and needed a little more life about me) and, most importantly, affordable.

The Yorkshireman in me likes a bargain and, while I wasn't buying a house to sell on in the future and intended to stay put a while, my budget was small yet, for some reason, I've delusions of grandeur and wanted a period property with tall ceilings, lots of light, original features and generous dimensions. I've always had a love of old and historic buildings and, combined with being chunky and quite clumsy, I am far happier when I've a bit of room to fall over myself in, with less likelihood of banging one's head (again!).

Eventually, I realised that property prices in Darlington were about 65 per cent cheaper than York like for like, and I found a grand, four-storey Victorian terrace, built in around 1850, sitting proudly above the road that, it would be fair to say, had seen better days (this may be an understatement). However, it was just in budget, available for the princely sum of £225,000 – not bad for something with 12-foot (3.7-metre) ceilings and 3,200 square feet (nearly 300 square metres) of light, bright, wonderfully built space.

My First Home

The house had been vacant for a number of years, and looked a bit like something out of a horror movie in places. It had been converted into an orthodontic practice on the bottom two floors, complete with a lead-lined X-ray booth, roller racking on the lower ground floor, air conditioning pipes running everywhere and plumbing from the dental chairs in the middle of all the floors. It also had the necessary fireproofing required for a commercial building (at the detriment to the original features) and, at some point, all the fireplaces and lots of the original bits had been ripped out. When viewing, I also thought the original cornice had been removed, but within an hour of getting the keys, some 'gentle' exploratory work with a hammer revealed that a false ceiling had been installed with the original coving still there – albeit in a very sorry state due to previous fire damage.

The top two floors had been turned into a duplex apartment, with its own access via a fire escape with a door where the beautiful, original arched sash window would once have sat over the original staircase. There was a boiler that looked like it was about to explode, a kitchen in the flat that had, at some point, been used to make the plaster of Paris moulds of teeth and was literally covered in the stuff, slightly creepy dentistry paraphernalia tucked into inaccessible places (the first used brace I found under some floorboards was a bit of a shock!), a bathroom resplendent with tobacco yellow walls and a rotten red carpet – and it would be fair to say it smelled a bit ... funky! It was a sorry sight, but I was outrageously excited about the whole thing.

I still vividly remember taking my folks to see it for the first time ... at this point, I'd still shown little interest in renovating, but buoyed by an enormous (and misplaced) sense of optimism and confidence, I felt sure the words 'how hard can it be' would see me right. Ma and Pa were, of course, endlessly supportive as always when it comes to my, um, enthusiasm for taking on a challenge (something they'd put up with time and again by this point), while making sure I'd thought through the consequences and whether, being really quite useless at such things, I was up to the task of renovating such a thing. Of course, my pals were slightly firmer with their opinions, all thinking I was quite foolhardy indeed.

Well, it turns out, it was quite hard ... but also hugely satisfying and, rather quickly, I found a huge thrill in using my hands for something practical and useful for nearly the first time in my life.

I realised that if I was going to go to all this effort in restoring the house as best I could, with countless hours scraping and sanding and covered in dust and detritus, I also wanted to try to learn a bit about design too. I figured painting the walls an interesting colour took the same amount of effort and time as painting them white, so why not do my best to choose something I really loved and that made my heart sing a little.

So, I started reading and spent hours trawling the internet. This was alongside spending my days at work, my evenings and weekends renovating, and often my nights searching eBay for baths, taps and toilets. The first room I tackled was, indeed, a bathroom, as the house didn't have a functioning toilet or anywhere to wash properly (and finances dictated I move in immediately while doing the work – there was no way I could have rented something as well). I wanted good-quality fittings that would last as I had no intention of having to redo anything anytime soon, but didn't have much of a budget. This was my first lesson: you would not believe what beautiful features people rip out of their homes – predominantly in affluent parts of London where there's many a bargain to be had if you know what you're looking for. The bath I chose for my

main bathroom would have retailed for over £3,000 and I paid £100 for it. It might have been used twice from what I could see!

The more I read and learned, the more excited I got... and, well, both the practical side of things and the design have become huge passions of mine and occupy an enormous amount of my time as I bring Admirals House back to life, but more on that in a bit.

My home in Darlington took just over two years to renovate, all while working full-time. I was immensely proud of what I'd managed to achieve, coming in on time and budget (both arbitrary figures plucked out of the air at the beginning really, having no experience at the time, but I was chuffed all the same), and creating a

home I loved and intended to then sit back and enjoy for a while, catching up on all the life you miss out on while renovating.

And then life threw a curveball. The company I worked for restructured (and there might have been a girl thrown into the mix for good measure), meaning I couldn't remain in Darlington if I wanted to stay with them, so having pretty well only just finished the final room, and never having gotten on to working on the gardens as I'd hoped, the house went on the market, I packed my bags and moved nearly 640 kilometres (400 miles) south to sunny Devon to work in their headquarters. It was a straightforward move. I sold the last place fully furnished. The buyers wanted everything

– the art, rugs, my TV and hi-fi, all the furniture, lights and even the house plants – so there wasn't a lot of packing. It was remarkably liberating and, given the option, something I would implore anyone to explore when selling their home if many of the pieces have, as they had here, been bought specifically for it.

So I trundled down to Devon with all my (meagre) worldly belongings, rented a tiny little flat by the sea and started looking for my next home. I'd definitely got the renovating bug by that point and knew I wanted a project – something old, interesting and, ideally, cheap (well, good value might be a better term ... no house will ever feel 'cheap' to me). My search was across a chunk of south Devon that needed to be commutable to

Buckfastleigh. I quickly realised that prices in most of Devon, as I'd found in York, wouldn't get me anything close to what I was hoping for (if I wanted to be anywhere near the sea at least, and it seem folly to move to somewhere famed for its coastline not to be). After lots and lots of searching, I found myself drawn to the remarkable city of Plymouth, for lots of reasons (namely house prices, some really beautiful Georgian and Victorian housing stock, and being the biggest city in the South West there was plenty going on too while still having the most incredible stretch of coastline, right on the border with Cornwall) which is where I quickly focused my search. It's there I eventually unearthed Admirals House.

ADMIRALS HOUSE

As soon as I saw this
Georgian lump, it was
love at first sight ...

As soon as I saw this Georgian lump, it was love at first sight ... as is, I'm sure, likely the case when you decide to look at the details of something on the market for double your budget. As is my (ridiculously unhelpful and illogical) want without even viewing the house, I used it as my benchmark to compare all other properties I actually could afford against ... and I found them wanting. Though way more affordable than many other areas of Devon, Plymouth was still dearer than Darlington, so it felt like a backwards step for me, which I really struggled with. I came close to buying a couple of lovely Victorian terraced houses, but was outbid at the last minute. The floorplans, description and history of Admirals haunted

my dreams though, so, on a dark, rainy night after work in January 2019, I found myself viewing Admirals – just to get it out of my system, of course.

Well, I could immediately see why it had been on the market for years without a buyer – it was absolutely knackered. There was water running down the walls from internal and external leaks; stagnant, overflowing buckets of water on one of the staircases supposedly once put down to catch said leaks; a variety of animals – some domesticated and others not – in the house; and parts of it that I don't think had been used at all since the 1960s. Parts of the house were inaccessible (indeed, it required an arch being cut through some plasterboard to access some of the rooms that had been sealed off)

In July 2019, I was the very happy, very excited and entirely daunted new custodian of Admirals House.

and the whole place was jam-packed full of 'stuff' – which is probably the polite way of putting it.

Of course, I didn't see any of that, not really anyway. All I saw was that she was MASSIVE, and gorgeous, and was absolutely crying out for someone to love her. But, more than anything, it amazed me then, and still does today, how 'homely' the layout felt. While it's undoubtedly a very large house, because it's over so many floors, when you're on any given floor, it doesn't feel that big. The rooms individually are generous without being cavernous. There aren't rambling corridors leading off into dark corners and, if you ignore the separate lower ground, and called the six rooms in the eaves on the top floor a fancy 'loft', then what you're really left with is a very spacious four-bedroomed house ... sort of (it's what I tell myself anyway and seems to work, with each of the three main floors simply being four or five rooms laid out around the central stairwell). I did some maths (badly) in an effort to convince myself it was doable, both in budget and in endeavour. Then, the next morning, with my heart pounding, despite knowing the offer would be rejected (being 25 per cent less than the asking price and some 43 per cent less than the house had originally gone on the market

for two years previously), I called the agent and let them know my interest, hoping that, once I'd been rejected, I could forget about the old girl and start focusing on properties I could actually afford, that wouldn't swallow me whole in the way a thirty-room lump could.

After a week or so of toing and froing, they came back with a counter-offer that I couldn't afford. Still, it wasn't a flat 'no' and a second viewing was booked (which is, of course, when all the negative points I missed the first time around became patently, and painfully, visible, not to mention about a million other things I hadn't noticed the first time around). I called the agent and explained that, rather than considering whether to increase my offer to meet their counter, I was now in two minds as to whether to withdraw my initial offer completely.

After significantly more deliberation, my offer of £485,000 was accepted and, finally, after the most stressful six months of my life with many, many ups and downs (including the sale being withdrawn entirely), in July 2019 I was the very happy, very excited and entirely daunted new custodian of Admirals House.

A Little Bit *of* History

Admirals is part of what was once the Royal Naval Hospital Stonehouse. Plymouth, as it's now known, used to be three separate towns: Plymouth, Stonehouse and Devonport. As the area's population grew and housing density increased, infilling the areas between until they became one, indistinct urban conurbation, in 1914, the three towns became the 'Borough of Plymouth'. In 1928, Plymouth was granted city status.

Plymouth has always been one of the most important naval sites in the country, even as far back as 1588 when it played a pivotal role in organising and supplying the fleet during the threat of the Spanish Armada, and throughout the eighteenth and nineteenth centuries the British navy was one of the largest and most powerful in the world. Built between 1758 and 1765, the Royal Naval Hospital was one of the finest medical facilities in Europe. Prior to that, sick and wounded seamen, when at shore from His Majesty's ships in Plymouth, had to make do with The Canterbury, a hospital ship kept in the docks (which was far from ideal, with additional accommodation made from old malt houses and empty sheds).

I'm incredibly fortunate when it comes to looking into the history of the Royal Naval Hospital here, that there are two brilliant books written about the site that have been a great source of information, quotes and pictures. One is by Surgeon Captain P. D. G. Pugh and called *The History of the Royal Naval Hospital, Plymouth*, written in 1972 (he rose to the rank of Surgeon Rear-Admiral and, in 1975, was appointed honorary surgeon to the Queen), and the other called *Up the Creek* by Graham Evans, who also served in the navy and wrote a fascinating book about the site both historically and as it transitioned into civilian use.

As for the care the seamen received prior to the hospital being built . . . well, it would likely make you squirm to think of it today. The lofts the sick lay in 'reeked with the odours of mortification and animals roamed the streets as if it were a straggling farmyard' and there was little in the way of actual nursing.

The building of the hospital came a few years after the one at Portsmouth (RNH Haslar), so lessons could be learned, and the eventual design was deemed of novel construction. Built on a 10-hectare (100,000-square metre) piece of land adjacent to Stonehouse Creek, a stone's throw from the sea, it's one of the first examples of a hospital built as a series of blocks, with a limited number of sick in each, and the blocks linked by a covered, open colonnade to help suppress the spread of infection and diseases. This style foreshadowed the pavilion style of hospital, which was to be made popular by Florence Nightingale a century later. There were 10 blocks (alas some were lost to bombing during the Second World War, during which over 40 bombs were dropped on the hospital site), that could house 1,200 sick and injured.

There's an incredible amount of history around the hospital site that I'll touch on as we go through the story of Admirals' renovation, but I think my favourite (being the simple creature that I am) is that the sick and injured were actually brought into the hospital by boat, coming from the sea and up Stonehouse Creek to a jetty just outside what is now my garden. The creek is now filled in and is playing fields, but, at the time, apparently it smelled pretty hideous so was known locally as 'Shit Creek'. With medicine not being quite what it is today, if you were too unwell to row the boat, your outlook probably didn't look too good and it's here the phrase 'up shit's

THE ROYAL NAVAL HOSPITAL,
STONEHOUSE, PLYMOUTH

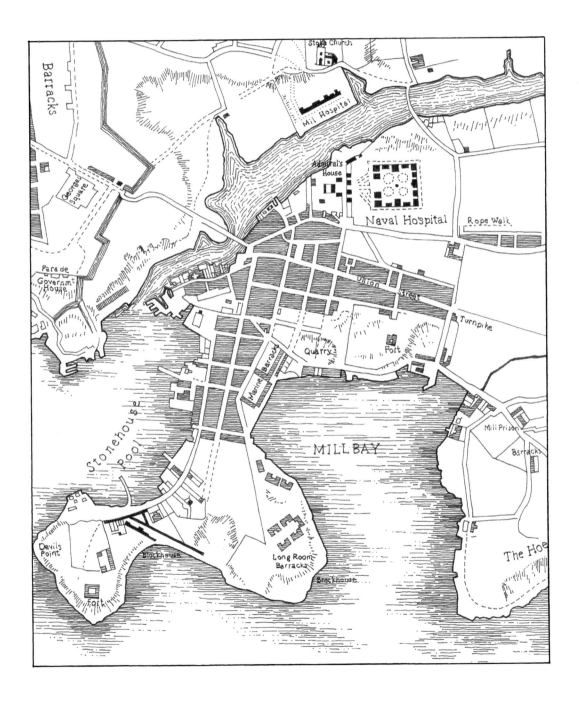

creek without a paddle' comes from.

Admirals House itself was built later, in 1804(ish), for Captain Richard Creyke, under his own instructions, by the architect Daniel Alexander Asher, notable for the early development of London Docks and, most famously, HMP Dartmoor, built around the same time as Admirals and still in use today.

Captain Creyke was appointed as governor of the hospital in 1795. Before then, the most senior officers on the site were the medical officers – who supposedly did a very poor job of running the place, despite being medically very proficient for the time. While there were nurses of a fashion, they were so lowly paid, and completely untrained, that it's said they left a trail of mischief behind them and were known for bringing in booze for the men and helping them to escape. Apparently, they would also steal the property of the dead and dying and were not above resorting to the world's oldest profession for an extra coin or two ...

One fateful day, upon which a sailor fell from some rigging on a ship and needed urgent medical attention having suffered serious injury, when he arrived at the hospital, not only were there no doctors to treat him, there wasn't even anyone on the gates to permit access. The sailor died of his injuries and an inquest was launched.

It turned out that the medical officers weren't really as disciplined as the navy might have expected and were off doing paid, private work instead of attending to their duties. After a board of inquiry was appointed which determined that a governor was to be taken from the list of captains in the navy, who knew the behaviour and habits of the seamen and could appoint proper, naval discipline, it was decided that Captain Creyke was the man for the job. On 16 July 1795, he went before King George III and was given the role.

Captain Creyke was described as an upright man of tremendous vigour (he was forty-nine years of age at this point, at a time when the average life expectancy of a man was around forty). Strict and God-fearing but humane and kind, he remained the governor until his death aged eighty, thirty-one years later, guiding the hospital through the challenging period of the Napoleonic Wars. It's said he only once missed Sunday

service in his whole time here and, on his first Saturday in office, made Sunday service attendance mandatory for his senior officers. A month later he banned all private practice by any naval doctors on the site.

It's worth remembering too that we were at war with the French at the time and life was hard. Creyke kept a diligent and detailed diary of which there are records, though, alas, only the first four years of his time at the hospital are known to still exist.

One excerpt, dated 11 December 1797, reads:

On the request of the Port Admiral, gave directions that two coffins shall be sent tomorrow morning to receive the bodies of the two mutineers of the Saturn, who are to be executed on board the Marlborough in Plymouth Sound.

Note, too, that this is the era of the press gang, and also the malingerer. The navy would both recruit by force and also take criminals and prisoners who would serve in the navy in lieu of their sentence (they'd likely have had a better time of it in the gaols!). To this end, the hospital site was built with an 18-foot (5.5-metre) stone wall around its perimeter which still stands to this day, not to keep people out but rather to keep others in.

Creyke wrote on 23 September 1795:

Two seamen escaped over the wall by means of a ladder left carelessly unlocked up. One of them is since taken in Plymouth, stealing in a shop.

On the 3 February 1796 he also wrote:

Report of the death of a patient who cut his throat in his bed this morning.

Prior to the building of Admirals in 1804, the only senior officers' accommodation was a row of four very fine terraced houses. Creyke, it seems, deemed himself worthy of something bigger and had Admirals built for

SIR HENRY F NORBURY, INSPECTOR GENERAL OF THE HOSPITAL IN 1895 AND THE 25TH RESIDENT OF ADMIRALS HOUSE, LOOKING RESPLENDENT AT THE BOTTOM OF THE STEPS THAT LEAD FROM THE ROOF TERRACE INTO THE GARDEN, AND YOURS TRULY LOOKING LIKE A WALLY RECREATING THE PICTURE 125 YEARS LATER. ON THE RIGHT IS CAPTAIN RICHARD CREYKE (1746–1826) FOR WHOM ADMIRALS WAS BUILT.

himself, and a visually very similar block built opposite that became the officers' mess and accommodation for junior officers.

It's worth remembering that Creyke would have been a very wealthy man for the time. In 1808 his annual salary was recorded as being £800, on top of which he had staff, the house and an allowance for running the household, for things like fuel, candles and food. Records show that, in comparison, the butcher employed at the hospital was paid £25 for the same period!

The Royal Naval Hospital would certainly have been a busy site. In the 15 years from January 1800, 48,452 seamen and marines were received at the hospital, and a great proportion of them returned to effective service compared to the days prior to the hospital's construction.

This busyness might explain why Captain Creyke deemed he deserved quite such a grand house, and household staff – not to mention it would have once been widely used for formal dinners and occasions, as goes with the role of governor of the hospital. To this end, throughout the entire 191-year history of Admirals prior to its private ownership, the officer in residence had at his disposal a private, full-time chef who would cater not only for him (for it was always a 'him') and his family, but also provide lavish suppers for the parties that were regularly thrown. And it is one of the greatest honours of my time here so far at Admirals House that I was fortunate enough to meet Albert, who served a succession of Admirals' inhabitants for the final thirty years of its naval tenure.

Meeting Albert

In September 2021, I was hand-delivered the most incredible letter, from a wonderful woman called Anne who had been running a group for men living with the challenges of Alzheimer's. In doing so, she became friends with Albert who, then in his eighties, was full of stories from his twenty-six years in the Royal Navy, followed by a further forty-ish serving as the personal chef here at Admirals House. Slowly, Anne realised it was this Admirals House he had been talking about, and the letter included a photo of Albert, in the house itself, shaking hands with Surgeon Vice-Admiral Anthony Revell in front of one of the fireplaces here.

Well, I was absolutely elated and we arranged for Albert, Anne and Albert's daughters, Carolyn and Lindy, to come for afternoon tea here. They were still keen to visit despite the chaos at the time – I was very much knee-deep in renovations. We had the most wonderful afternoon and they were kind enough to bring lots and lots of photographs, not only of Albert cooking in the little kitchen here, but of his wife, Pamela, who also worked as the housekeeper for a time and of Carolyn and Lindy playing in the house and garden, as they would often do whenever the resident officer was away. I've shared some of the pictures here.

Albert would often find himself cooking formal dinners for sixteen, which is remarkable given Admirals had such a tiny kitchen, and I think it speaks of the playfulness of his character that there are pictures of him 'borrowing' the officer's uniform one day for photos in the garden.

Whilst his memories were a little jumbled, Albert was able to tell some wonderful stories of the house and its inhabitants, and spoke very fondly of his time here, despite working six days a week. Even Christmas dinner was cooked by him in the morning, before he headed home after the main course was served to be with his family, leaving clear instructions on how to prepare pudding.

He told me of going shopping, usually with 'the lady of the house' who would decide what they wanted that week, to pick up provisions. He was also responsible for keeping the wine cellar stocked and would have to decant gallon containers of spirits into smaller bottles (occasionally taking a nip to 'test' whether it was any good or not!).

Albert spoke very highly of (almost!) all the officers, and indeed an Admiral Howson and his wife became godparents to Carolyn and Lindy, and remembered picking mulberries from the ancient tree in the garden.

He was certainly a little dismayed at the state of the garden (frankly, who could blame him?), but it was such a joy to meet them all, hear their stories and give Albert a bit of time back in his old 'office'. They also gave me a treasured gift – a plate Albert had kept hold of, from the formal chinaware used in the house, which was very kind indeed.

The room he used as the kitchen, which was still the kitchen at the time I bought the house and which will one day become a utility/laundry/boot room, will always be known as Albert's while I'm at the helm of the old girl. I trust he'll approve of the work I do in there, once I get around to it.

The whole surrounding space is now known as 'The Millfields' and it's a conservation area so it's all protected, and much of it is listed.

Admirals House *Now*

It's remarkable that the Royal Naval Hospital remained so for the navy (and many locals too) right up until 1995, when they sold the whole site to individual private buyers. The officers' accommodation has all remained residential, the old wards are primarily now apartments with some business use too, and there's even a school on site. The whole place is now known as 'The Millfields' and it's a conservation area so it's all protected, and much of it is listed (Admirals is Grade II listed). It all looks remarkably like it would have done 200 years ago, with very little change.

The original building of which Admirals is now a part has been split, with the right-hand third of it, as you're looking at it, a completely separate home. (Though it's very hard to find any solid evidence of when this was done, it must have been a very long time ago – my guess is the early 1800s after the death of Captain Creyke.) So, the Admirals I own is actually only two-thirds of the original building.

The building would have been a very large property as one. Even split, Admirals is now across 5 floors, with 8,200 square feet (762 square metres) of accommodation and 30(ish) rooms, including staff quarters in the attic. There are around 100 internal doors, 60 windows, 17 fireplaces and a lifetime's worth of restoration required.

The navy were not always, shall we say, the most sympathetic of owners, though, thankfully, unlike some of the other houses here that had been used as offices and for other uses and therefore boshed about a bit, Admirals has always been someone's home.

Of course, in the military, a home is not quite the same as it is for anyone else. Between 1826 and 1972, there were no fewer than 52 different heads of the hospital, all of whom would have lived here. That's an average of two years and nine months of residence ... so it wouldn't have had quite the same TLC as it would have

All in all, Admirals was in a very sorry state.

if someone had owned and loved it. Given the very significant layers of paint on everything, it feels as though every time there was a new officer in charge, a team would steam through the whole house, slapping a layer of paint (badly) on everything to give it a 'freshen' up (a neighbour, who was also in the navy, did say to me that the navy's approach was along the lines of, 'If it moves, shoot it; if it doesn't, paint it', which certainly seems fitting here!).

As changes were made to modernise the house, little thought was given to the character or architecture – a brilliant example of which was a radiator, likely installed in the 1960s, that had been positioned directly in front of a beautiful, original fireplace. This would have been bad enough, but in order to fix the radiator to the wall, they simply drilled straight into the marble surround. For someone like me, keen on preserving the history of buildings, this is hard to fathom, but I guess it is understandable given the nature and use of the house. Of course, the person doing it may have not known it was gorgeous Carrara marble, as, just like everything else, most of the fireplaces had been painted in countless layers of beige gloss paint.

When I first bought her, Admirals was in a pretty bad way (there is, as always, a silver lining as had she been in good condition, there's certainly no way I could ever have afforded her); very little had been done in the way of maintenance since the building had transferred into private ownership. One of the most significant causes of water damage was a simple blocked gutter from a birds' nest and, within ten minutes of getting the keys, I'd been out one of the loft windows and onto the roof. It was a bit of a reach, but I was able to clear it – this alone, had it been done years before, would have

saved countless damage. Another leak was from a cracked shower tray on the top floor that had remained unfixed for years and the back door to the house was actually off its hinges and propped up in the garden for some mysterious reason, which certainly didn't help matters with a cold gale running through the house and was, shall we say, an interesting security risk.

The first thing I did when I moved in was run around to check whether the aforementioned 'stuff' had gone ... it was my biggest worry – it would have cost untold thousands to remove it all myself, so I'd made it very, very clear that, if it wasn't gone, I would have to pursue things legally. Thankfully, nearly everything was indeed cleared – even the straggly roses planted amongst the weeds in the back garden had been ripped out.

There were, though, fire extinguishers, left over from the navy's ownership, dotted about the place and, in parts of the house, there were still laminated signs from the 1980s stuck to the walls with instructions of what to do in case of a fire, untouched since the navy's departure twenty-five years previously.

A friend who saw me the afternoon that I got the keys hadn't ever seen my usual unflappable demeanour be quite so rocked as it was that first day I moved in. I think it was the smell more than anything – it's hard to describe, but all I can really say is that you should be grateful some of the pictures in this book aren't of the 'scratch-and-sniff' variety.

However, seeing the house empty for the first time, and into rooms I could barely step into when I viewed it initially, was very liberating and the possibilities and potential were huge. At the same time, though, the real scale of the task at hand hit me.

WHERE I STARTED

I'd sold all my worldly belongings with my last home

First things first, given the state of the place when I moved in, I needed to make it feel a little habitable in the medium term before I could even begin to think about the main renovation. None of the toilets functioned properly and the hot water had a mind of its own – Admirals really was full of treats! On top of that, as I'd sold all my worldly belongings with my last home, and the little flat I rented was furnished, I had no furniture. Luckily, I managed to find a cheap, second-hand sofa that day from Facebook Marketplace so I had somewhere to sit and a room was cleaned and a camp made with a bed for that night.

Next up was to clean ... and try to eliminate the smell. I had a friend who needed a place to stay with his children, so the lower ground floor, which had, in part, had some work done to turn it into its own apartment with bathroom and kitchen (albeit badly, that will, in time, need redoing from scratch), needed cleaning and making a bit more habitable too.

I needed to get at least one of the bathrooms and toilets functional, and also set to work restoring one of the fireplaces in what is now the main living room, removing the hideous 1980s inset fire, repairing the original marble surround and installing a wood burner (as you'll come to see, wood burners are one of my favourite things in all the world). I nearly fainted when I was told by the energy company what they wanted to set my direct debit to – it was more in two months than I had spent annually in my last house – so getting a form of heating sorted that was efficient, and controllable, only heating the space I needed, was imperative.

I also had to work out the hot water system, which was set with an uninsulated 28-millimetre loop around the house from the vented hot water tank in an outhouse. This partly explains why some of the bills were expensive, as it seems the boiler was on 24/7 – even when you didn't use any of the water. As there were pumps sending it around this loop across four floors of the house, by the time the loop returned, it was stone cold, and would turn a full tank of hot water cold in a couple of hours ... while very convenient, it was absolutely bonkers. So I installed new hot and cold lines up and down the height of the house, ready to tap into as I eventually got on to the various bathrooms throughout the house. I roped in my pa to help with some of the longer runs that I needed an extra pair of hands for, leading to a memorable, very cold (alas, not for the right reasons) New Year's Eve with no hot water.

The whole place needed rewiring too. Of course, it would have been far easier to do this in one go, but as I'm living in the house throughout the renovation, this isn't really practical – there was also no way I could have worked out where everything was going all in one fell swoop (nor afford to do the work in one go), so the rewire is being done one room at a time, and one floor at a time, which means it's broken into manageable sections.

Once I'd got some of the basics done, and had a space to sleep, wash, eat and cook (on a single, plug-in induction camping-type hob which did me proud for four years!), it was time to start cracking on with the work.

HEATING AND FIRES IN A DRAUGHTY OLD GEORGIAN HOUSE

Firstly, if you're considering taking on a big lump like I did and feel the cold – and don't have very deep pockets (like me!) – it's important to recognise that it's nearly impossible to keep these old things warm, like lots of people have become used to in more modern housing. The idea that the whole place can be 21 degrees Celsius, all year round, without bankrupting yourself – on my budget at least is a folly … so, you have to adapt your thinking around warmth slightly and also how you live, just as the Georgians would have done all those years ago.

I will caveat all these things by saying, firstly, I run pretty warm and don't really suffer when it's cold. One year, the house was around 5 degrees, other than one room with the wood burner in, and while I wouldn't say that was fun or even all that comfortable, it was, more or less, fine for me. Secondly, hailing from Yorkshire which is known for getting a bit chilly, Devon, and specifically Plymouth, nestled right by the sea, is very, very mild in the winter most years (bloomin' wet, mind you and, typically, the winter I decide to sit and write a book rather than work up a sweat renovating, it is unusually cold), which definitely helps when trying to get things warm(ish).

My approach is similar to how everyone used to live really, going right back to when we lived in caves – centring life around a fire. It's one of the reasons I love an open-plan space so much … add a fire – or, more specifically, a wood-burning stove – and you can effectively heat that one space in which you spend 95 per cent of your waking life when at home.

As I mentioned earlier, installing the wood burner in the main living room was one of the first things I did to the house. I'd had a wood burner in my previous home and I loved it so much I knew I wanted the exact same one here – it's hyper efficient, but, just as importantly, it's beautiful, with an incredible view of the flames. I find it really hard for a place to feel like home without a fire – I have tried it and didn't like it one bit. They're so much more than the warmth they offer … they're a companion, a friend. My late grandmother lit a fire in her hearth in her living room every single day, all year round, right up until she passed in her mid-nineties. It needs looking after, nurturing, but show it some love and it responds, burning hot, bright and efficiently. A fire adds atmosphere in a way that nothing else can. I genuinely believe, after thousands of years with the fire as the absolute centre of our homes, we're conditioned as humans to be drawn to and comforted by it. Watch as people enter a room how quickly they gravitate towards it. The smell, the flickering flames … it all adds up to a focal point for life.

Fires are not without their drawbacks, however. If you burn good-quality, sustainably sourced and thoroughly dried hardwood (beech, ash, hornbeam and a little oak are my preferred choices; birch can work, too, but it burns fast and hot, so doesn't last quite so long and therefore, despite being a little cheaper, usually doesn't work

out as good value), it doesn't come cheaply. It also requires significantly more effort than flicking the thermostat and can introduce dust into the home. Fires do also require a level of operator competence to get the best out of them and its imperative you get your chimneys regularly swept. The best stove in the world, run badly, will be a smoky mess while giving out little heat. But when it's running well, there's little to beat it.

There's been quite a lot of information, and misinformation, around the environmental impact of wood-burning stoves. I am not an expert, but I do believe a high-quality, modern wood-burning stove, run well on good-quality, dry fuel by someone who knows what they're doing, is a sensible way to heat a home like this. The fuel source is, of course, renewable, unlike gas or coal, and with the new rules around emissions, they really are extraordinarily efficient. The problems come when

people burn damp wood or, worse still, whatever they have to hand – plastic, cardboard, you name it – so there is an onus on the owner to burn responsibly. I have spoken to an expert on green energy and, with the current technology, there just isn't a better solution for Admirals, or indeed I imagine in many older houses – especially one that has restrictions on it. Solar panels wouldn't be allowed anywhere here and an air source heat pump would be monumentally expensive to run – and likely be unable to get to an adequate temperature anyway unless the radiators are swapped over to be so big as to be impossible to place in the rooms. A ground source heat pump would also be out of the question due to cost and location. I'm hopeful that, eventually, technology and investment lead to an increase in green electricity production and we can use this electricity to make these homes, with their lack of insulation and their single-glazed 200-year-old windows, comfortable and affordable to run. They will only survive if people can live in them (and love and cherish them), and something does at some point need to change to enable this to happen.

Personally, I prefer wood burners over multi-fuel models. I only ever burn wood anyway, and these models tend to be better for that purpose rather than trying to do both not quite as well. Using only wood means they're harder, though not impossible, to keep in overnight, but, with a modern stove, in this country at least, I believe that's unnecessary anyway (and bad for the stove/chimney) given how quickly and easily they light and get up to temperature. Mine are from Dovre and locally-based Stovax, and are some of my favourite things in the house.

With the wood burners in the key rooms, it means my reliance on turning central heating on is significantly diminished, and I'm only heating the spaces I'm using. Obviously, there are some occasions when a little heating might be needed, if I've got guests coming over, for example, or a blast in the bathroom is needed to chase off any lingering moisture from a shower. With this in mind, I've installed all the radiators with digitally controlled, Wi-Fi-enabled thermostatic valves. This isn't the sexiest topic in the world, but they're brilliant. Mine are from a company called Wiser, and they basically allow me to do a similar thing as I do with the wood burners and only heat the spaces I need. At the push of a button (on my phone), I can turn the heating on only in the bathroom. It keeps all the other radiators closed off, so the loop only has to go from the boiler to the bathroom. Obviously it's not 100 per cent efficient, but much, much better than the system trying to heat up all the radiators in the house (I haven't counted them up, but I would guess there will likely be around fifty by the time I'm done). It also means I'm able to turn the heating on and off from my phone anywhere in the world and control the whole system from it. It's definitely an investment at the start, but one that will pay for itself many times over in the long run.

As for heating a space with an open fire, as much as I adore sitting next to one in a cosy pub – the sound, the smell, there's nothing quite like it – I think in 99 per cent of cases, it's quite hard to justify due to how incredibly inefficient they are and their environmental impact. (If you do have them, though, please retain them – or the surrounds at least if you're adding a wood burner – where possible.) If you think about your fuel source, it has a certain amount of calorific value within it, no matter how you use it, but the appliance you use it on determines how much of those calories are turned into heat and, in turn, passed into the space you're actually trying to warm up. With an open fire, only around 20 per cent of the calorific value of those very expensive logs gets used in actually heating your space; the rest goes up the chimney. Not only that, but with huge amounts of warm air from the room disappearing up the chimney, any warmth from your radiators suffers the same fate. Conversely, wood burners are around 80 per cent efficient for modern burners (an 'A' rated gas boiler in comparison is 90 per cent plus), so are night and day in their difference. They don't have quite the same ambience, but on every other measure they're better, safer, cleaner, more environmentally friendly, warmer, more efficient … it really is a no-brainer. If you 'room seal' a stove (where the air used to fuel the fire comes directly from outside) they're even better as you're never using the lovely warm air you've created to run the stove and then see it disappearing up the chimney to be replaced with cold air from outside.

If you've got fireplaces that you don't use (such as the ones here in my bedroom/bathrooms), it's worth investing in a chimney balloon or similar for them. This stops the gales blowing through them, but still allows some airflow to stop any dampness, and if they're chimneys/fireplaces you won't ever use, it's worth capping them off (again, ensuring there's adequate ventilation) to stop rain – and birds – coming down. In uncovering one of the fireplaces here, I found no fewer than seventeen bird skeletons – a messy job, and a fairly grim way to go too!

SHOULD I RENOVATE?

I believe a lot of what I've got to say applies regardless of the size of the project, though of course the bigger you go, the longer it'll take and the greater the risks involved.

Before I talk about the rooms individually, and some of the work I've done, I wanted to mention a word on renovating. While I'm no expert, I thought it was worth offering a little insight into the whole thing for anyone out there who might be keen on doing something similar. I believe a lot of what I've got to say applies regardless of the size of the project, though of course the bigger you go, the longer it'll take and the greater the risks involved. These thoughts certainly aren't aimed at a property developer or someone looking to flip a house for profit – it's not a world I know about. Admirals hopefully will be my forever home and it's to that end I'm renovating it.

Of course, there are also different levels of

'renovation' too ... it's a bit of a catch-all term for all sorts, from a lick of paint and perhaps a new bathroom and kitchen at one end, to something so riddled with dry rot there's naught but the walls left by the time you're done: two very different prospects. The type of house you look at will also have a significant impact on the type and level of work involved. A classic Victorian terrace is a glorious thing. Often beautifully put together out of straightforward materials, there are thousands of them across the country and they are familiar. Missing fireplaces and similar are easily found in salvage yards and the construction is known by most people so they're easy enough to work on and are unlikely to throw up surprises (there are, of course,

always exceptions to a rule). Any task you need to do on them you'll likely find countless videos on YouTube or examples in DIY manuals showing you what to do, on buildings that look very similar.

On the other hand, you might be looking at a fifteenth-century cottage with cob walls made from unicorn tail hairs and the tears of fairies, with a thatched roof and a waterwheel to generate power, located on an isle in Scotland accessible only by boat when the tide's in ... It's unlikely that you'll find a plethora of tutorials online on how to restore such a thing, nor can you pop down to your local builders' merchants for a bag of unicorn tail hair. Similarly, there's a reason why that castle you saw online for the cost of a bag of peas is priced like that – as tempting as it might be when scrolling after a glass or three of wine to sell up and move to your own fortress.

The first point I'd like to make, though, is that renovating is intensely rewarding – massively so – and that's certainly the overriding thing I take away from it. I renovated out of necessity (if you can call it that, given it's caused by the aforementioned Lordship complex and not wanting something more within the realms of 'normality'); I didn't have the money to buy

the house I wanted 'done', nor did I have the money to pay someone else to do the work, and necessity is, of course, the mother of invention.

There are people out there who are extraordinarily generous with their expertise when it comes to sharing information via YouTube, Google, blogs, and so on – all for free. There's also a wonderful community I've found myself a part of on Instagram, full of like-minded people all going through a similar thing, which really helps as it can sometimes be a bit of a lonely existence.

However, renovating certainly isn't for everyone, and for every person who absolutely loves it, there will likely be ten who think it's an absolutely ridiculous thing to do. While a lot of the work is fairly straightforward and isn't technically that difficult to get your head around, and is definitely within the realm of learning how to do on a DIY basis, it is very tough indeed, so I urge you to go into it with your eyes open.

First of all, it's physically demanding. Doing DIY day after day, you'll ache in places you didn't realise you could ache, your hands and knees will take a real battering and, alongside setting myself on fire, I've

more cuts and bruises than you can count at any given time and I've even managed to give myself mild lead poisoning (but more on that later). Risk of injury is also high (it's easy to skip the health and safety precautions professionals would take when doing it yourself), especially when you're tired and stressed; and it's likely that you'll be cold and wet a lot, so it helps if you're physically robust. Your hands, and grip strength in particular, come in very useful too.

Your diet will likely suffer as well – when you're working that hard, and it's cold and you've no kitchen, the last thing you're going to want to do is start peeling carrots and eating a wonderfully balanced, nutritious meal, even if you know you should. Again, I can only talk for myself, but ease and comfort rank highly, as do things that can be cooked in one pot ... and it's remarkable how good a beer tastes when your throat is dry with dust.

Then there's the mental toll it can take. I'm sure lots of us have seen a few episodes of *Grand Designs* and the big things that can go wrong (though it's worth keeping in mind that it's a telly show, and apparently drama makes for better TV than plain sailing), but, more than that, it's the daily grind of it – living

through it – that shouldn't be underestimated. The cold definitely wears you down (see the aforementioned 5 degrees throughout the house) and the dust gets everywhere. It can also put a strain on relationships and friendships. Money is a fairly constant cause for concern for most of us (though, of course, renovations come in all shapes and sizes, and to people with different means), and there'll be more than one sleepless night, anxiously waiting for the plumbing you just finished to go pop, or wall tiles to come crashing down just as you're drifting off.

It is bloomin' hard – I really can't stress that enough – so if you're able to get yourself in a place where you can throw yourself at the renovation because the other parts of your life are relatively settled and you're operating well within your capacity, you're probably giving yourself a better chance of success. Things like being stable in your work/job/business and, if you have one, being comfortable and settled in your relationship really do make a difference. I probably wouldn't recommend planning a wedding/baby/major career move in the middle of a renovation (though lots of people do).

Budget, *or* lack *of*

For most people of normal means (of which I very much count myself), I think it's really important to have an eye on the longer-term plan – or more specifically the longer-term plan B, should plan A not work.

While I very much hope that Admirals is my forever home, and that's absolutely the spirit in which I'm renovating it (I'm not sure any property-flipping TV programme would ever recommend eighteenth-century wallpaper everywhere, for example), without the benefit of a crystal ball, who really knows what the future might hold – an injury or illness, a family member needing care, what I do for a living needing to change, needing to move to a different area for work ... there are lots of unforeseen reasons beyond my control why I might need to move on (albeit with a very heavy heart). For me, that means it's important to do your utmost to never find yourself in a position where you've spent more on a house than it's worth. Others will disagree, or may have a different motivation (or simply enough in the bank to be able to cover it and not worry about such things), but I personally feel like I should be able to walk away if I really needed to without an unserviceable debt (or even just the crippling angst I'd feel if I'd made some decisions I know I'd regret).

With that in mind, it's really important to do your sums when you're looking at a property that needs renovation. Indeed, it's a significant factor as to why no one had taken on Admirals in the years it was on the market; financially, it just didn't stack up, unless you're doing the work yourself (and, even then, if profit was my motivation, I'd have been much better off buying small terraces and flipping them). While I'm all for falling in love with a place (indeed, there's no way anyone could do this without that pull),

letting your heart rule your head completely, puts a financial burden on you that, I think, on top of everything else a renovation is likely to throw at you, may be the straw that breaks the camel's back.

Of course, it's all well and good telling you to do your sums, but budgeting for a renovation is notoriously hard, and the bigger and older you go, the more unknowns there are. For me personally, it was a case of looking at what I could do myself versus what I'd need to pay people to do. I didn't care so much about the amount of work needed or the time it was likely to take me. What was far more important to me was whether I'd be able to do it with the very modest skills I had (but huge enthusiasm to learn more) rather than having to pay people to do it ... even if it takes me fifteen years (and likely the rest!).

Another big element is understanding the work required and being honest with yourself about what's possible for you to do. For me, this meant that I would have likely walked away from anything very structural and especially anything showing serious rot – in particular dry rot which is quite prevalent here in the south-west of England. Dry rot requires ripping out everything affected by it, and the areas beyond, and redoing it. When you're talking about floors, ceilings, walls, staircases – maybe even roof trusses – taking a building of this sort of size back to its bare stone walls and rebuilding, well, that's a task I just don't have in me on this scale, both in skill, money and endeavour, especially when you're talking about a listed property and the restrictions you face (even when the work is necessary to actually save the building from further damage). That is work that is technical, complex and, certainly with a building like Admirals, far beyond my skill set. Of course, nothing is impossible, but the cost and effort of putting something right properly,

that's that far gone, especially when it's listed or protected, is absolutely not to be underestimated – in the case of Admirals, if it had serious dry rot, the renovation could have cost more than the house would ever be worth.

Listing is also something to consider. Again, I walked away from a number of properties due to their listing because their existing layout didn't work for me. While that can be altered, it takes a significant amount of effort, cost and expertise, and there's still no guarantee (and rightly so in plenty of cases) that you can make the changes you might want to make. Admirals suits me beautifully as it is in terms of where doors, walls and windows are, so no structural changes were needed to make the house work for me in the way I live here and use the spaces. Mainly, I'm simply sympathetically restoring what's there or, in some cases, putting back what's missing, and anything I'm adding – the kitchen, for example – could be removed one day with no real long-term impact on the building. I see myself as the custodian of Admirals, for as long as I'm here, leaving it in a better state than I found it, hopefully to last another 200 years and more. Equally, I'm not a fully signed-up member of what I (affectionately) call the 'hair shirt brigade', for whom restoration is almost a dirty word. There are some, to me it feels, who would rather see buildings go to ruin, than be carefully modernised to make them comfortable for modern living. Houses and buildings typically evolve to suit the occupiers' needs at the time – Admirals is no different. It was carved up, the staircases changed, the Victorian era extensions added, doors moved and removed, the lower ground, once the beating heart, all but abandoned as staff levels reduced and modern conveniences of gas-fired boilers and cookers used, central heating added (sometimes inappropriately!) ... These aren't museum pieces, but there's definitely a balance to be struck. Obviously, with a listed property there's very little you can remove, but even with something non-listed, but old, I would always implore you to think very carefully before removing something of historical value that can't be put back.

The final thing to consider is whether you're looking to extend. Again, while not impossible to DIY, and one day I might rather like to have a go at building from scratch, it comes with a boat load of complexities and costs, even when DIYing. You might come up against regulations that require you to upgrade bits of the building you're not touching for it to meet regulations, including insulation and issues around fire safety, and so on, which can cause real headaches.

If you can find a property with a footprint that already suits you, you're far more likely to keep control of the budget from day one, with fewer hidden costs and pitfalls to come across – not to mention the hassle and heartache of the planning process, the cost of architects, surveyors and structural engineers, and inevitably the tradespeople you're likely to need.

Having said all this, to remind you of my first point after lots of doom and gloom: with the right attitude and aptitude, renovating a home can be the best thing you'll ever do.

ROOM

by

ROOM

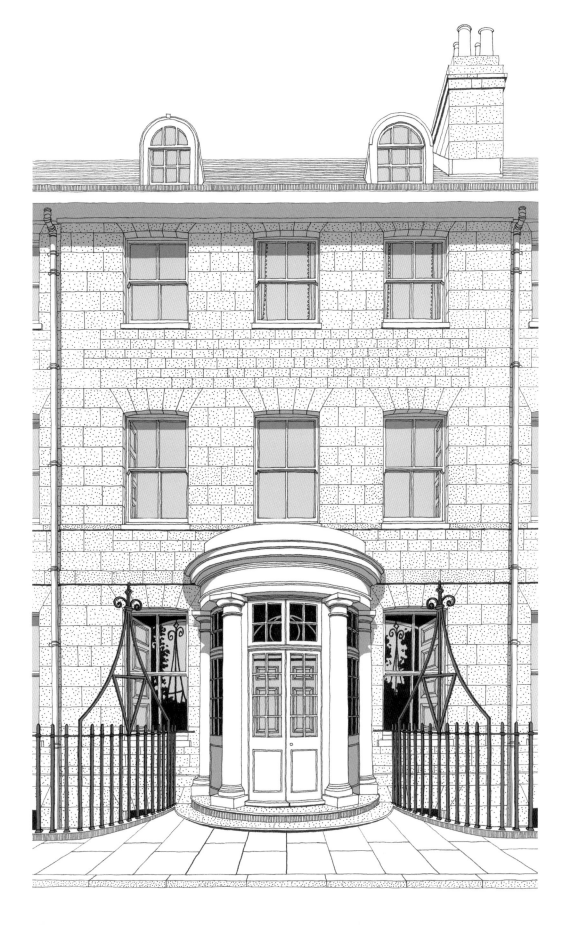

THE
FLOOR
PLANS

Floor plans are always the first thing I look at whenever house hunting. They tell me far more than the pictures can as to whether the space will work for me and the flow and feel of a home. I hope that these help you to find your way around Admirals as we go through, room by room, without getting too lost!

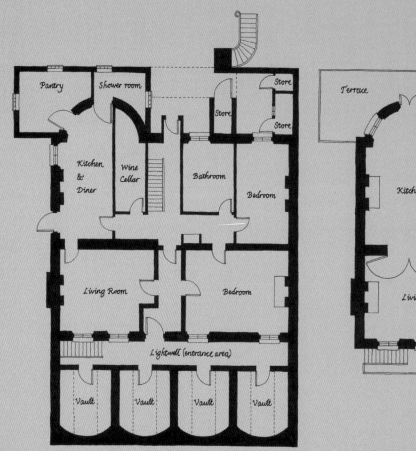

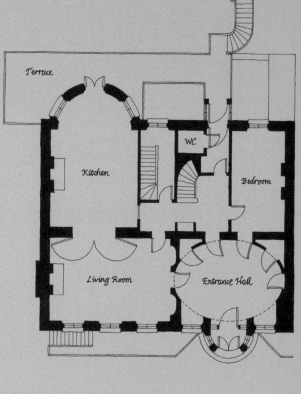

THE LOWER
GROUND FLOOR

THE
GROUND FLOOR

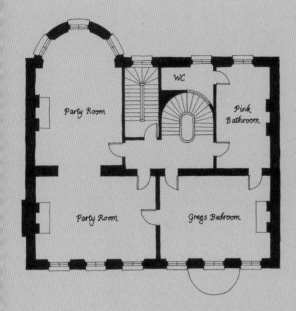

THE
FIRST FLOOR

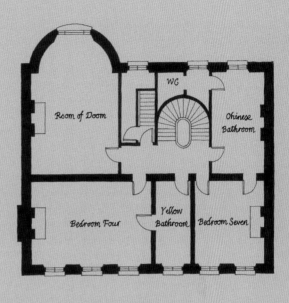

THE
SECOND FLOOR

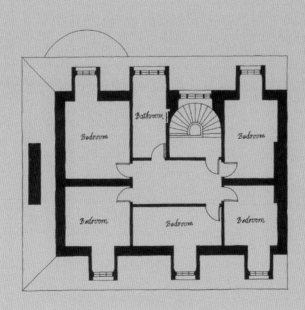

THE
THIRD FLOOR

The
GROUND
FLOOR

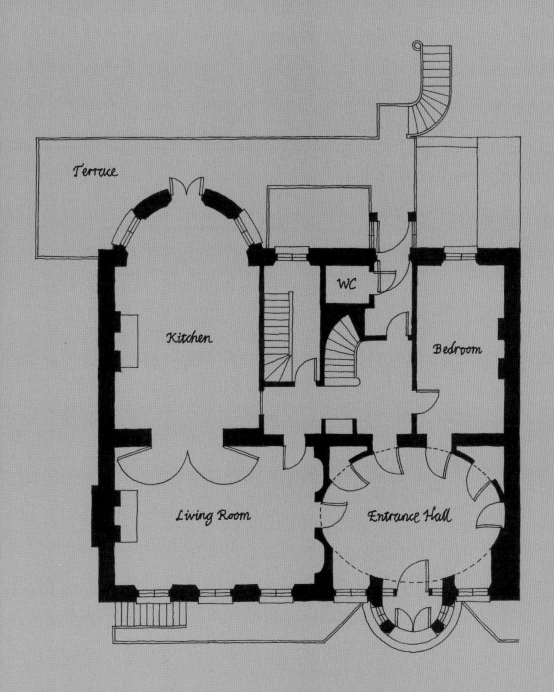

Terrace

Kitchen

WC

Bedroom

Living Room

Entrance Hall

Ground Floor Plan

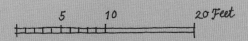

5   10   20 Feet

The
ENTRANCE
HALL

Possibly my favourite room in the house, architecturally at least, is the entrance hall that the front door opens on to. A perfectly elliptical room, hugely wasteful in terms of its use of space, but appropriately Georgian in wanting to impress in an elegant and understated sort of a way; it would have been massively labour-intensive to create.

Through *the* Looking Glass

YOUR FIRST STEPS
INTO THE GROUND
FLOOR OF THE HOUSE

With its six internal doors, all curved to perfectly match the walls, the entrance hall feels like something out of *Alice's Adventures in Wonderland*. To add to the mystery and whimsy, when I started work on this room, only three of the doors actually opened.

As I started to strip back the paint and uncover their secrets, frankly it was all a bit of an anti-climax. One had a very slim cupboard behind it and would, I believe, once have been the door that took you from the hall into the part of the building that's now a separate house. The door next to it was more curious, though. I knew it didn't lead anywhere (the room on the other side of it has a cupboard with a solid, curved back), but curiosity got the better of me and I had to open it up.

Well, I was the first person to see behind that door since the one who installed it over 200 years ago ... the hinges were present, but decorative, not attached to the door itself, and the whole thing was nailed into the frame. The back side of the door had been left rough-sawn, totally unfinished, and rather than some kind of buried treasure, the space behind it simply contained the skeletons of a few mice that had decided to make it their final resting place.

Behind the third door, once I'd removed the obstructions, there was ... another door – this one leading to what will one day be the 'butler's pantry', with both rooms having their own door, one curved, one flat. There's a space about 15 centimetres deep between them, though the door of the pantry doesn't actually currently open and is yet to be investigated, but I believe it's due to some very poorly laid tiles.

Of the three left, one is a cupboard, so only two of the six internal doors, intricately curved at no doubt great expense by His Majesty's Royal Navy, actually went anywhere! Still, they look rather splendid and would have been suitably (if subtly) impressive as the first room in the house Captain Creyke's guests would have seen – they also took forever to restore (only a slight exaggeration).

This room took a bit of doing. On the surface, it looked to be one of the rooms in the best condition. Alas, the surface was a filthy liar. It's a similar story to all the rooms really – layer upon layer of wallpaper and paint, unsympathetic previous tradesmen – and it all needed peeling back with lots to repair and sort. It was the paint-stripping in here that nearly finished me off – literally (ish – I'm being a bit dramatic) – as I gave myself lead poisoning with all the paint scraping, something that caused me to change the way I strip paint in a far safer way (see page 116 for some tips on doing this safely).

There was months of work just to get the woodwork back to bare wood, and I didn't dare remove any of the curved doors as, remarkably, they all still fit beautifully and I was certain, once removed, they'd never go back on quite the same – so everything had to be stripped in situ – and, of course, as you strip, you uncover rot, damage and missing bits, so getting it all to this point took an absolute age. Again, radiators had been boshed into spots that ruined the look of the room, so I relocated them to below the windows, so the walls can really sing now, especially with the wallpaper.

THE WOODWORK FELT LIKE A NEARLY ENDLESS TASK AND TOOK MONTHS, BUT THE END RESULTS WERE WELL WORTH THE EFFORT

It would have been massively labour intensive to create. There are 6 internal doors, all curved to perfectly match the walls, which is especially incredible given that when I started work on this room, only three of them opened.

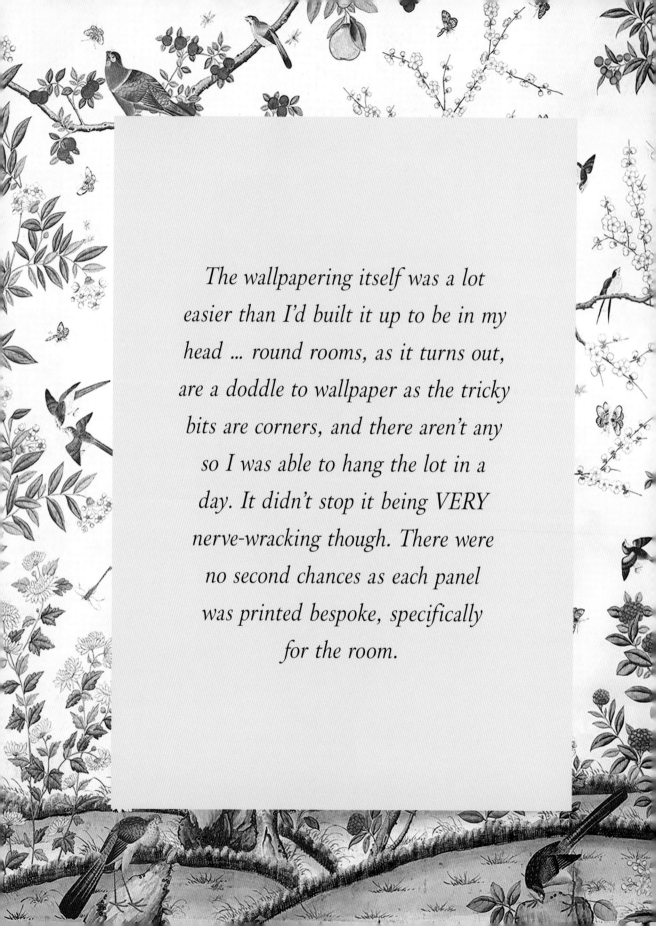

The wallpapering itself was a lot easier than I'd built it up to be in my head ... round rooms, as it turns out, are a doddle to wallpaper as the tricky bits are corners, and there aren't any so I was able to hang the lot in a day. It didn't stop it being VERY nerve-wracking though. There were no second chances as each panel was printed bespoke, specifically for the room.

Wallpaper

Outside the house is 'the square' – a sort of quadrangle of houses that would have made up the senior officers' accommodation, all built around (ironically) a round lawn, on which are cherry blossom trees, and this is the view out of the windows of the entrance hall.

These were the inspiration behind the way I decorated in here, with a beautiful, faithful, digital replica of an eighteenth-century hand-painted chinoiserie (a decorative style characterised by Chinese motifs, blending European designs with East Asian artistic traditions) from Zardi & Zardi. The wallpaper wraps around the room, without a repeat across any of the panels – either in height or across the circumference – and, when you walk in, it's like you're stepping into a beautiful, mythical forest. It adds a wonderful atmosphere when there are people around for supper.

It also makes quite an impression, as would have been the architect's original intention when designing this room, when people enter the house for the first time.

The wallpapering itself was a lot easier than I'd built it up to be in my head … round rooms, as it turns out, are a doddle to wallpaper as the tricky bits are corners, and there aren't any so I was able to hang the lot in a day. It didn't stop it being VERY nerve-wracking though. Unlike normal wallpaper, where a mistake just means an annoying bit of waste as you cut another piece from the roll, here there were no second chances as each panel was printed bespoke, specifically for the room. It was also the first time I'd ever used an overlap and then cut through method for joining them, which, again, was much scarier than anticipated, but worked a treat.

Flooring

The flooring is an aged, mid to dark oak that was created bespoke by Broadleaf Timber and made in Wales to order. They liked the finish so much that they actually introduced it to their range – and called it 'Admirals Oak', which made me very proud indeed! It is designed to give the feel of an oak floor that might have seen 250 years of use, with warm bronze tones balanced out by some greys to give it the age. The darker floor grounds the space beautifully, and is also the perfect foil for any rugs or furniture above it. It's very clever in its construction too: it's solid oak, but, rather than a single solid board, which may be prone to some movement, especially given the house gets very cold in winter and very warm in the summer in the south-facing rooms, it uses three layers. It's all still solid oak, rather than the more usual layers of plywood, so it retains its density and character, but the middle layer is set across the grain making it far more stable.

Furnishings

The entrance hall is a really lovely space to be in, with the walls wrapping around you, and it felt far too nice a space to simply pass through on the way to the rest of the house without pausing to admire and enjoy it. At the same time, with its many doors and windows, and novel shape, it's impossible to do very much with it in terms of use and furnishings. There's also no fireplace to give it its natural focal point (or much-needed warmth).

In the end, I decided I would add a table that mimics the shape of the space, plonking it right in the middle of the room. On a day-to-day basis, it has no chairs around it and simply functions as a large 'hall table', atop which sits a huge vase with some foliage in, and one day, erm, objet d'art, which is far too fancy a word for me – you know, pretty 'stuff' – so it creates a nice welcome to the house as you come through the doors. The table in the middle also forces you to linger ever so slightly, rather than walking directly across the room, and gently guides you to one side, flowing through into the living room, rather than the rear, more workman-like part of the house.

For occasions that demand it, like Christmas dinner for the years I'm hosting, I add chairs around the table, and it becomes Admirals' formal dining room. I appreciate it isn't used all that often, but it's rather nice to have such a special room reserved for occasions such as this, and its shape definitely lends itself to such a use. As I'm editing this very chapter, I've just hosted the first Christmas here (*see page 66 for more on this — and some lovely pics*).

There's still plenty for me to do in this space – it needs a rug (easier said than done given the shape of the room), some window treatments (again, not entirely straightforward given they're within deep panelling) and a few finishing touches, but it never fails to make me smile whenever I come home.

As with everywhere, there's rot and damage and all sorts of treats to look forward to that I've yet to tackle.

The Front Door

One of the biggest things I tackled as part of this space was the front door, so it feels worthy of its own little section ...

I knew stripping the paint from the whole porch would be hideously messy and likely ruin the finished entrance hall, so, to protect it somewhat, I stripped the door and its frame at the same time as the hallway. I thought I best at least paint the door again, to both protect it from weathering, but also to keep things looking a little smarter as you come into the house.

I'd been following a brilliant, professional painter on Instagram called Wesley Knight (@wkpd1986), who's incredibly generous with his knowledge and expertise and from whom I've learned lots. He'd done some doors in a super-high-gloss finish, which I think looks extraordinary. All the exterior woodwork at Admirals is in brilliant white gloss – totally inappropriate for the period of the house (brilliant white paint wasn't available

until after the Second World War, so, in my mind, has no place in an 1804 house and something softer would feel far more authentic). Having stripped back the paint, I know that, once upon a time, the woodwork would have been a very dark green, which would look absolutely incredible. Modern oil-based paints also aren't great for external woodwork, causing rot and damage. However, given all the houses around the square are the same, it's something I'm stuck with. I always knew, though, that the door wasn't staying white (well, a sort of grubby beige is what it really looked like, having become very tired), and would need fully stripping. As there were so many coats of paint, it had obliterated all the beautiful carved details.

So, with some advice from Wesley and bundles of overenthusiasm in my abilities, I set to work, trying to recreate this super-high-gloss finish. Now, the question most people ask when they see the finish is what paint

was used, but in reality, it's not the paint that gives the glass-like finish – not in its entirety anyway, though of course using a good-quality oil-based paint is important. If you put that on anything less than a near flawlessly smooth finish, though, it's never going to give you the same effect. Once again, the prep work was key here, and very intense – firstly filling all the holes, dents and cracks (with the associated sanding back between) and multiple layers of primer. Then I went over it with something called 'gras a lacquer', which is an oil-based, very slow-drying filler, that you have to put on in layers very, very thinly, with 24 hours between coats for drying before sanding back. These layers build up, hiding all the imperfections and unevenness in the grain, and, eventually, give you a surface to add the paint to that feels like glass.

Then, it's a case of adding a few layers of the gloss paint – again with a full day between to dry, and sanding with very fine grit between layers. I warmed the paint in hot water which helped it flow on more smoothly, taped all the internal edges to stop any bulging of the paint and rolled it on before laying everything off with a special, super soft laying off brush, and also did everything I could to keep the air around it as free from dust as possible – I'm fortunate that there's a porch that can be closed, both for security on an evening so the front door can be left open, but also to keep the wind at bay (don't even think about doing this on a breezy, dusty day).

All in all, it took forever, but it worked – and I absolutely love the end result! It's so shiny I can actually use it as a mirror to check the state of my visage as I'm heading out. It also looks a bit bonny with a Christmas wreath attached – even if the rest of the porch still needs an outrageous amount of work.

IT'S CHRISTMAS!

Christmas is one of my favourite times of the year and I wanted an excuse to put lots of festive photos in the book, so I'm including a short section here on getting into the festive spirit.

I like to think Admirals is rather a good house for Christmas; Albert's daughters told me they used to love Christmastime here, as there would be lots of grand parties they'd sometimes be allowed into, as both their parents would be working here. They remember carols being sung in the oval entrance hall too – perhaps the acoustics are especially good in there?

With lots of rooms, and lots of fireplaces, I'm nearly spoiled for choice with what to decorate, and have moved things around most years – seemingly getting more lavish (and possibly ridiculous) every year, but it was absolutely incredible to have the house full of loved ones on Christmas Day for the first time in 2023. After years of hard work, that really felt like the cherry on the cake and a huge reward. Even better, the house worked perfectly – it was the first time I'd ever used the entrance hall as a dining room, so I wasn't totally sure how everything would flow or what it would all feel like to be around the table in that space, but it was so, so lovely. The room worked just as I'd hoped and was the perfect backdrop to a very long, very boozy Christmas dinner.

With the wood burner lit, the Aga fully up and running, and, as a special treat, the radiators on too, it was lovely and warm in the house too, so it really did feel luxurious. The living room was the perfect space, between the kitchen and dining room, for people to gather and chat while I was running around finishing the food and, well, I couldn't have been happier. I wonder where I'll put the trees this year.

I like to think Admirals is rather a good house for Christmas; Albert's daughters told me they used to love Christmastime here.

A FEW GLIMPSES OF
CHRISTMASES OVER
THE YEARS SO FAR
AT ADMIRALS

The
KITCHEN

THE

GROUND

FLOOR

The kitchen is one of the most recently completed rooms – and for good reason. I'd have loved to have completed this room much earlier, but it's fair to say that beautiful kitchens don't come cheap, and I simply didn't have the budget to do it earlier in the project. Instead, I concentrated on some of the less expensive rooms to complete, such as the bedrooms.

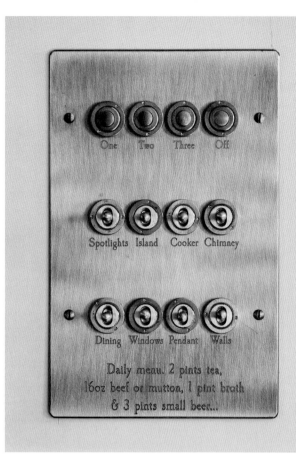

A lot *of* Hard Graft

THE HEART OF
ADMIRALS HOUSE

Now, the kitchen as it is today is a far cry from how it looked when I first took the old girl on. The formal dining room had seemingly been left to be used as a cat's play room – with the associated smell soaked through the ancient carpets and into the floorboards. Indeed, one of the first things I did was clean out the fireplace hearth of what I assumed was old ash and embers. Upon closer inspection, though, it was lots of very well-used cat litter dumped in there – one of the sources of the aforementioned bad smell.

The double doors had countless layers of paint on them that all needed stripping off, the chimney breast was wet from a leaking chimney and serious rot had set in, so it needed taking down and rebuilding. The marble fireplace mantel had broken in two, so I had to remove the whole fireplace in order to repair it and carefully reattach it (thankfully, I managed to do it without breaking anything – no mean feat when working solo as they're jolly heavy). The radiators were knackered and had been put in the most ridiculous places, and there was rot around the windows from the leaking gutter I'd climbed out of a window to fix. The windows needed refurbishment, and the whole lot rewiring and making safe.

It was within this room (once the formal dining room) that I found a foot-operated servants' bell – not original as it was electric, so it would have been part of the second round of staff bells that were added (the first were mechanical, sadly long gone; the only evidence of them being the wires and pulleys beneath the floor). With its lead-sheathed wiring, I'd guess it was installed in around the 1930s. I've actually spoken to people who had fancy, formal dinners here under its ownership by the navy, and no one could fathom how the staff knew the perfect time to come in and clear plates the second the last diner had finished their meal, or when someone needed a top-up ... discretion being the order of the day back then clearly!

Now, we generally live without staff and, alas, we're left to fend for ourselves. Certainly for those who like to cook (and eat, which you can probably tell from my, erm, stature, that I very much do), the kitchen is the heart of the home, so the layout for me was really important.

Layout

As I've said, the space at Admirals, and the layout, was actually one of the many things I first loved about it, having already got spaces we'd probably refer to as 'broken plan' nowadays, namely on the ground floor. (Broken plan is a version of open plan that allows a little more flexibility – with areas zoned and with the ability to either partly or fully close off or shield certain parts, with doors, sliding screens, shelving, and so on, to help change the way you use the space.)

The two principal reception rooms on this floor, one at the front and the other at the back, of a similar size, are separated by a set of double doors, 10 feet across and 10 feet tall (3 by 3 metres), that, when open, allow for an 'open-plan' feel, but are definitely two rooms that helpfully have the option to close the doors – though it's very unlikely I ever will; they're so big it would mean moving the sofa!

The room I chose for the main kitchen was the back reception room. By carefully relocating the main kitchen to the back room and putting a small, day-to-day dining space within it, leading through to the living room at the front of the house, with the doors open, it is, for all intents and purposes, an open-plan space.

This room also has a set of double doors in the centre of the bay window that lead outside onto a very dilapidated roof terrace, with old stone steps going down into the garden. (The garden at the back of the house is lower than the street level at the front, meaning that the garden drops away at the back.) The terrace is large enough for a table and chairs for al fresco dining, with a beautiful outlook over the garden when the sun's shining, without being far from the kitchen. It is, of course, in need of a huge amount of work, but, eventually, will link the kitchen to the outside beautifully.

Design

As for most people, the kitchen has become the most important room in the house for me. Of course, originally, Admirals' kitchen was on the lower ground floor and strictly the preserve of the household staff. Sadly, the original kitchen and features like the range cooker, storage and pretty much all of the old character down there have long since been ripped out. However, it's incredible to think of what that lower ground space would once have felt like – a hive of activity at all hours in the belly of the house, ready to meet every whim those upstairs might have, with food and drink being sent up via a dumbwaiter added, I believe, in the Victorian era, with a 24-foot-long (7.3-metre) wine cellar, ensuring no one ever went thirsty.

I don't know for sure, but I believe the kitchen then moved upstairs, on to the ground floor in a small-ish room (around 16 by 10 feet/4.9 by 3 metres), in the 1950s. I assume that it was likely around this time, or during/post the Second World War, that the volume of household staff would have been thinned significantly, and a more modern kitchen was installed that was capable of being run by significantly fewer people. Here, it would have been Albert in the kitchen and a housekeeper – often Albert's wife. Again, as per the stories of Albert earlier, the Admirals here would never have done something so common as cook for themselves, so the idea of a grand kitchen, or at least one in the more formal areas of big old houses, is something of a modern invention. Even in houses far larger than this – proper stately homes – the kitchens, while large, would still have been the preserve of the staff and were placed strategically for a number of reasons, whether to stop the spread of fire to the main house, should one break out in the kitchens, or in a north-facing part of the house, to keep temperatures cooler despite the constant fires burning in the hearths.

There are a few things that had a huge impact on the specific design of Admirals' kitchen, as well as some wider points to consider when designing a kitchen. I will be the first to admit that, despite being a very enthusiastic (I use that word rather than 'good') cook, who loves to while away hours over a hot stove, there are choices I made that sacrifice a little convenience for beauty. The same thing can be said for the whole house really.

First up, the room has rather a lot of architecture within it that can't be changed without consent that may or may not have been granted (not that I would have ever considered changing it for a moment – I'd far sooner sacrifice outright practicality to keep the beauty and history of the space). The large fireplace, a semi-circular bay window that is 20 feet (6 metres) across, the aforementioned double doors, a further 'normal'-sized door, nearly 12-foot (3.7-metre) ceilings with cornice and an enormous central ceiling rose don't make installing your usual kitchen entirely straightforward.

Being an open-plan space, I also didn't want the kitchen to feel too 'kitchen-y', which I know may sound absurd, but it's the same for bathrooms too. I've never understood why spaces like living rooms and bedrooms are often warm and interesting, and yet, when it comes to kitchens or bathrooms, everything becomes hard or clinical and often not very friendly-feeling. I appreciate

This is a work of romance, not necessarily of practicality.

there's a level of practicality when it comes to areas where you create mess or get clean, but sterile spaces bring me absolutely no joy, even if they are easy to dust. This also goes for appliances or the ugly clutter that often comes with a kitchen (and I don't mean a beloved collection of recipe books or vintage copper jelly moulds) – no one will ever convince me that their electric kettle, air fryer, or whatever the latest new-fangled kitchen gadget might be, is attractive. While this might not matter in a kitchen that is solely a functional kitchen, unconnected to a living room or dining space and never used for relaxing or entertaining, in a space that's used for so much more than cooking (I've written this book at my kitchen table, for example), I think it's a really important point.

The first thing for me to do was see where in the room I could actually fit the kitchen in while respecting and celebrating the original space. Once I knew where things could go, it was then a case of cross-referencing that against my wish list of what needed to be in there. At Admirals I'm fortunate in that the old kitchen Albert once cooked in, situated just across the hallway, will serve as what I've already referred to as 'a butler's pantry' as I'm hoping, one day, to have it crammed full of beautiful storage, resembling somewhat the wonderful old spaces full of crockery, china and silverware you see in the grand stately homes of Britain. It will also serve as an 'overflow' kitchen, given that I can't – nor wanted to – cram the main kitchen with huge amounts of stuff and storage, which would have inevitably taken away from the lovely bones of the space.

Once I'd worked out the basic layout, I pretty much ended up with the same design I had in mind before I even viewed the house for the first time. Howard Stubbs, kitchen-maker extraordinaire with an attention to detail the likes of which I've never seen, then helped me create a design, based around traditional Georgian cupboards and furniture, that would feel right at home in the space, and cleverly hide all the fussy appliances behind closed doors, so they were within reach and easily used when needed and mercifully out of the way when not.

The design included a central island and, while I'd have absolutely loved a traditional work table on legs, there just wasn't the space to get all the appliances against the wall to facilitate such a leggy design. Similarly, I didn't want a fully solid island, as the sight lines through the space, in particular when sitting down, through the doors and out over the garden would have been lost, and I think it would have felt too heavy in the room. As a result, a design based on a bath dresser was created, with a dresser base style to the front of the island, which is most visible within the room, and, on the back, opposite the cooker, the units go all the way to the floor, hiding the dishwasher, a pull-out bin, the sink (and associated detritus held within) and a wide, deep set of drawers for cutlery and crockery. Under the dresser, there's a shelf made from reclaimed oak, older than Admirals itself, which has been the perfect place to store and display large platters and what not. Howard brilliantly referenced the pillars by the front door portico when turning the legs for the dresser side of the island out of solid oak.

ALBERT'S KITCHEN

This room is currently chock-full of my tools and general detritus, and will be one of the last rooms I do at Admirals. As much as I'm itching to get on with it, it's always useful to have a rough, unrenovated space where possible, for washing paint brushes and what not, without worrying about damaging or ruining anything you've already worked on. It's on the ground floor, and is of course where Albert did all his cooking, hence the name! By the time I'm done with it, it'll work as the utility room, laundry room, boot room and overflow storage for the kitchen. I'm rather grandiosely referring to it as 'a butler's pantry', though I'm not sure, strictly speaking, that's entirely accurate.

Remarkably, Albert did all his catering on two very conventionally sized cookers, both tucked under the enormous, commercial grade hood coming out of the chimney breast. At some point, a modern, chipboard, plastic-wrapped kitchen was added, with faux wood Formica worktops … needless to say, there's an awful lot to rip out in here. There are also a lot of holes in the walls and floor from services coming up from the boiler room and into the rest of the house which are going to need carfeul investigation – as well as the inevitable restoration of all the woodwork and the usual rewiring and plumbing to sort.

It's a room I'm ridiculously excited about though. I'm not sure why, but I, like lots of people, seem to be intrinsically drawn to these hard-working rooms. I remember talking to a volunteer at a National Trust house, and they said people are always far more fascinated by the working rooms than the grand, stately ones. I think it's because most of us (myself very much included) can relate to them far better, knowing if we'd have been born 200 years previously, these are the rooms we'd be seeing far more of.

The absolutely brilliant Howard Stubbs, of Heaven and Stubbs, and I have been working on the designs for this room, and he's then able to turn them into these incredible, and very realistic, CGI images to give you a flavour of what it will look like – one day!

Even though it's going to be a very hard-working room, I still want it to look beautiful. As the hall that leads onto it is very dark, the door will likely often be open to allow light through into it, and with it being a place where coats and shoes will live, guests will definitely see it too. The plans will be refined a little nearer the time, but it'll look something like this: lots of storage, an inbuilt bench seat and lots of hooks for coats, and, on the other side, in front of a window, will live a big, salvaged Belfast sink and lots of shelving, with a Victorian clothes dolly above to dry bedding. The washer and tumble dryer will be stacked, with a pull-out shelf between to rest the laundry basket on (laundry is one of my least favourite chores so I'm all for anything that makes the task easier – Howard did suggest a laundry chute from the bathroom above, but that feels much too fancy for me!). Next to this will be a full-height wine fridge, beside another full-height fridge which is an overflow for the kitchen fridge (it'll be my beer fridge – I'm very, very excited!). The walls will be panelled to protect them from knocks, meaning I can use them to hang all sorts of useful bits and pieces, and I'm hoping to include a little secret compartment somewhere too.

On the chimney breast (sadly any fireplace that would have once been here is long gone) will sit a free-standing dresser that will be used to store, and display, a rapidly growing collection of platters and tableware, and should be a really lovely focal point as you enter the room. Hopefully the whole thing will have the feel of those beautiful rooms you see in stately homes. At the very least, it should be a slight improvement on the purple plastic cabinets currently in place!

The Oven

Behind the island is a run of units within which the beating heart of the kitchen sits: an extraordinary eighty-ish-year-old Aga cooker. The Aga was salvaged and fully restored by Blake & Bull near Bath, a family-run business that saves these wonderful old relics and makes them fit for modern life – much like what I'm trying to do with Admirals. The Aga has been completely stripped back and sand-blasted down to the original Coalbrookdale Foundry cast iron, and then re-enamelled, before being rebuilt around new, modern internals and insulation. Old Agas are, undoubtedly, a thing of beauty and, having had them in the past, there's a strong sense of familiarity and nostalgia about them (the only house I ever knew of my grandparents on my ma's side – a small farmhouse in East Yorkshire – had a wonderful pre-1972 two-oven model that my grandmother, despite not being

a particularly keen cook, absolutely adored right until she passed in her early nineties; it kept the kitchen cosy, and her many, many dogs happy over the years, and was a very faithful companion). I was, however, very conscious of the running and environmental costs, which are usually very substantial, regardless of the fuel they use.

Fortunately, with a modern conversion, they are fully controllable, beautifully insulated, easily turned on and off and much, much cheaper to run while still being a gloriously cosy thing to perch your backside on in the winter. The thing I love most, though, is that, despite all the technology and cleverness now included within them, they have still retained the absolutely classic look they've always had. All the controls and LED panels are tucked away behind the door through which coal would once have been fed.

Cabinets

In my opinion, the kitchen is one of the places where, if possible, and especially when you're looking at a home you're creating for yourself to live in for a while, you should splurge a bit. The difference between a handmade, bespoke, in-frame kitchen and a mass-produced flat-pack one is absolutely enormous in almost every way apart from price, as remarkably they're often not as much as you might think. If I take my last kitchen, the cabinetry cost less than it would have from any of the more well-known high-street kitchen shops. I then found appliances second-hand or 'seconds', because of damage to a side that you'll never see once installed that saved thousands.

By going down the bespoke route (assuming you go with a reputable cabinetmaker with lots of experience, of course), you're getting a kitchen that is far more beautiful to look at and is made of better quality materials (mine is made from solid English beech), which means it will not only last almost indefinitely, but also get better with age as it wears and patinates. If you fancy a change in look, it

can be repainted time and again, and you can even update things like handles, cornice and mantels to really make it feel like a different kitchen. All of this means they're far more sustainable in the long run and will likely work out cheaper too if you're staying put.

There are lots of ways you can keep the costs down too. Reducing the volume of cabinetry is the easiest thing to do. In some initial draft designs of Admirals' kitchen, there was a huge bank of wall-mounted cabinets going right up to the ceiling. While these would have been beautiful, in reality, they weren't really necessary as I had enough storage elsewhere, and taking them away significantly reduced the cost of the kitchen. Fewer, beautifully designed pieces rather than cramming as many cabinets in as you can is definitely worth considering and can make the difference between getting something beautifully handmade versus mass-produced.

More than anything, though, having a bespoke kitchen really allows you to make the most of the space, creating cabinetry that fits perfectly, utilising every spare

inch without fillers or gaps, as well as creating a kitchen that works specifically for you. For me, being a bit taller than average at 6 foot 2 inches, but with almost comically short arms (I can't touch my elbows together across my chest and am affectionately – ish – known as 'T-rex' by some; the only other person I've ever met to not be able to do the same is my dear pa), having a standard 90-centimetre worktop would mean I'd be hunched over when chopping veg and would end up with a sore back. In Admirals they're at 98 centimetres, which eliminates this issue. It also means that everything is set perfectly where I'd want it, with every detail agonised over … there's a pull-out, concealed drawer that has sectional storage for chopping boards, above which is a magnetised, solid oak knife drawer for my beloved Japanese cooks' knives. The cupboard below the sink, usually a mess of bottles, cleaning items and waste pipes, has a deep, pull-out drawer that keeps things neat and tidy. It really does make the kitchen an absolute joy to use.

Of course, good things come to those who wait and these things take time – not just in coming up with the design and details, but in the crafting of it too. It's fair to say that I was also WAY more interested in every single detail than most. It was a running joke with Howard that I wanted to know absolutely everything and, of course, had an opinion on it all too. Most of his clients tell him vaguely what they want and he comes back with the design. Whatever end of this spectrum you might be on, if you want something handmade, specifically for you, rather than something mass-produced and off the shelf, it's worth starting work on it earlier than you'd think.

On the opposite side of the kitchen, with the beautiful fireplace, there sits two arched cupboards, again designed to reference classic Georgian furniture and retain the symmetry within the space. One is a deep pantry for food and, on the right of the fireplace, where the alcove is very shallow due to the bay window, there's a drinks and glasses cabinet, slimmer at the top than the bottom so it doesn't block the light or view from the window.

Worktops

When it comes to kitchen worktops, as is my preference for nearly everything in the house, I'm not a huge fan of 'faux' anything, much preferring the real thing for its beauty and authenticity. The space I had available dictated that I needed to have the sink in the island, meaning that wooden worktops, while possible, weren't the best idea given the inevitable issues around water – there are ways around this, with stone inserts and similar to minimise the damage, and wood is endlessly refinishable, but it's certainly less practical. So, in this instance, stone was needed instead. Most people at this stage go for a quartz or similar, and for good reason – it's a remarkable material; it's very resilient, stain- and heat-resistant, consistent, stable and easy to work with. The best quartz is pretty much impossible to tell from the real thing in look too (I couldn't pick which was the real marble from the samples when I went to choose my worktops – it's hugely impressive).

Marble, on the other hand, is porous so it can stain. It also reacts to acid, like lemon juice or tomatoes, which can etch the surface. Being a natural material, it can contain flaws and cracks that might not present themselves until the last minute as it's being installed in your kitchen, but goodness me, there's nothing that glows quite like marble when the light hits it and, as incredible as quartz is getting, I don't think it'll ever quite match the real thing for me.

That wasn't the reason I chose marble in the end, though. I intend to live here for a long time – the rest of my life if I'm lucky – and I've absolutely no intention of ever replacing this kitchen, or the worktop, short of a fire or a flood forcing my hand. The beauty of marble, to me at least, isn't that it's super stain-resistant, or super strong andchip-resistant or similar ... it's the fact that, yes, while these things happen, when they do, they often add to the beauty of it, rather than detract from it. Again, it's a personal choice, but I can't imagine anyone ever looking upon a 250-year-old Italian Carrara marble fireplace, with its wear and stains, and thinking anything other than it's utterly exquisite. Michelangelo chose it for his David; it just feels ... right in an old place like this. And while there are lots of fancy, heavily veined, striking marble options out there, I think the subtle, soft beauty and colours within Carrara marble are perfect. Even better, the marble used for my worktops was sourced by Algarve Granite through Imperial Stone Group from a quarry that is a 'co-operitivo', meaning it's owned by the workers so everyone gets fairly treated. I actually got to visit where it was being cut and turned into my worktops too – a fascinating process – and I was able to choose the edge profile as they had samples for me to feel. My worktops are 30 millimetres thick; modern kitchens often have a 20-millimetre top, but that feels slightly out of proportion in a traditional kitchen, especially one made taller like this one. A square edge felt a bit hard and unforgiving, so I chose the soft curve of a bullnose for my worktops and absolutely love them. The curve makes a huge difference to how tactile the island top feels when you're leaning against it and has saved more than one plate from smashing when I've knocked it against the edge clumsily.

The guys at Algarve Granite came to template and actually created, by hand, the vision I had for the splashback, with its gentle curve either side of the Aga, all made out of a huge, single piece of marble. It's a really fascinating and skilled process that needs a very steady hand and was a joy to watch. Helping the guys get that massive, heavy but quite thin and therefore fragile piece in, above the Aga (which is far too heavy to remove of course), was one of the most nerve-wracking moments of my life!

Another bonus with this marble in particular is that it's quite cost-effective, so all in all it's a win for me and, at the time of writing, in the six months or so that it's been in and used, yes it's marked, etched, and there's even a chunk out of an edge where I was being especially clumsy, but all these things are just adding to the aged, lived-in feel I was hoping to achieve.

Some musings on wooden worktops

In my view, solid timber, when done with beautiful wide staves to show off the grain and character, is a brilliant choice for kitchen worktops when they are away from a water or heat source (I couldn't use them either side of the Aga either due to the heat). Yes, they mark and age, and need the occasional oiling, but, for me – just like with marble – that's part of their charm … but then again, I like old things and find my antique furniture charming and beautiful with its wear and patina, whereas others might want shiny and new. If that's your thing, then a quick sand and oil gets them looking as good as new. Wood is also cheaper than stone and, for an island with neither cooker or sink on it, as my folks' last place had, it makes for a wonderfully warm, forgiving surface around which to congregate. I think it's always best, where possible, to go for a wider stave versus the bitty effect you get from the narrower sections. It costs a little more, but it's there you really get to appreciate the grain and character of the wood and see the craftsmanship evident within it.

Hidden Gizmos

There's a hot water tap in the island. I've never had one before, and thought it might be somewhat overhyped – surely boiling a kettle isn't such a hardship – but having now lived with it for a while, I wouldn't want to be without it. It's so convenient, particularly with a house full, as well as saving space on the worktops and keeping things looking clean and tidy. If you're not sure as to whether you should go for one, do it.

An integrated fridge-freezer, that still has an ice maker and water dispenser just like its American cousins, looks like a big old cupboard from the outside, and the dishwasher is hidden away too. There's also a pantry to the right that hides the combi microwave oven, and things like the coffee machine complete the run, with beautiful scalloped pan drawers hidden behind cupboards either side of the Aga. The pantry door has a spice rack, so, when cooking, the door remains open, tucked against a wall so it doesn't get in the way and gives me access to everything effortlessly.

Lighting

I've dedicated a whole section to lighting on page 106, but lighting a dining kitchen can be tricky, needing to work for a multitude of uses – from getting through a mountain of veg prep to a gently lit intimate dinner – so I just want to touch on it here. It's common to see a huge grid of spotlights littering the ceiling in kitchens with wanton abandon, which, in my 'umble opinion, doesn't feel right in an old building, and it's rare you need all areas lit with exactly the same intensity. Not that spotlights were even an option here – I don't think the original lath and plaster ceiling would have taken too kindly to me drilling a load of big holes in it and likely would have deposited itself upon the floor (and on my head). Equally, I think it's important to ensure light levels can be bright enough so that one doesn't cut one's thumb off with some enthusiastic onion chopping after a glass or two of wine!

The starting point for the kitchen lighting actually came from an old picture of the hospital wards here in the hospital. They had beautiful, possibly gas-powered, lights – a long, elegant twin arm design coming from a single point. Ever since seeing that image, it's what I'd imagined above the island, but, despite searching, I hadn't found anything quite right. Melissa, who runs Lumière du Jour, was then serendipitously at a lighting trade show in the US and saw a wonderful brass light that echoed the lighting I loved so much, in a timeless but slightly more contemporary style, even meeting the designer there too – it all felt meant to be.

After that, the rest came together beautifully. All the lights are controlled on independent, smart dimmers that look like old-fashioned solid brass toggle switches, but work perfectly to dim everything as needed as well as being controllable from my phone. I even engraved the daily menu of the sick and injured staying at the hospital in the 1800s as a little nod to the hospital's past – they ate (and drank) rather well I thought!

The dimmers allow me to set the mood of all the lights with either the touch of one button or just by speaking to Alexa, and I've used lighting to create 'zones', such as a beautiful alabaster pendant over the dining table, separate zones around the fire and around the cooker, and then some discrete bar lights on the ceiling providing some ambient, directional light. This gives more than enough light for prep and cooking, but feels wonderfully cosy when dining or entertaining. As well as spotlights, I'd be wary of having too many bare or visible bulbs in any room, but especially the kitchen – they're often so bright they can dazzle unless dimmed to the point of ineffectiveness.

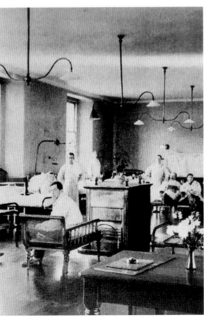

Finishing Touches

In terms of colour and pattern, again I didn't want the space to feel too much like a kitchen, and wanted it to feel coherent and in harmony with the semi-attached living room, but not to decorate the spaces identically. I also needed to acknowledge the north-facing light in the kitchen and decorate accordingly.

The first thing I chose (beyond the layout, which we've already discussed) was the wallpaper. I went for a small-scale block print – 'Lilou' from Warner House, which is based on an eighteenth-century Kashmir shawl in a soft blush colour. Not only does the colour give warmth to a room with predominantly cool light, but the small print, when viewed as a whole, disappears slightly and seems to just give the walls a warm depth and texture. It's incredibly effective, and I actually paired it with the same print, in a different colourway, in the living room, which I'll come on to.

I already knew the floor covering, as this was flowing through from the hall, and will be the same throughout the ground floor.

The cabinetry is painted in muted, soft tones, again grounded with a very dark brown/black island (and pops of blue inside the pantry cupboards, which is a little bit of a fun surprise). Given it's a kitchen that will outlast me, I first of all wanted to choose colours that wouldn't date, and would also work with nearly anything else given there's a good chance the room will be redecorated before the kitchen needs repainting. They also work beautifully against the pale marble, and again add a warmth and softness to the space. Using the same colour on the alcove cupboards as I've used on all the woodwork in here ('Sheringham Beach' by Fenwick & Tilbrook – a soft, off-white-y stone colour) helps give the impression that they might be original Georgian cupboards and frame the fireplace with near symmetry.

Dark oak internals again are timeless and tie into the floor, and the aged brass hardware matches the original brass found in the house in the form of the hinges and doorknobs. After that, it was simply a case of accessorising with some patterned fabric in the form of blinds and cushions for the window seat, and a few other little finishing touches, and I'm thrilled with the results.

The wallpaper's small print, when viewed as a whole, disappears slightly and seems to just give the walls a warm depth and texture.

OPEN PLAN: SHOULD I OR SHOULDN'T I?

*In my mind, the benefits
of having a space that is
open are huge.*

For full disclosure, I absolutely love open-plan living spaces as they just work better for how I like to live, so perhaps I'm a little biased. I am merrily child-free, which means there's not really a reason for me to need separate spaces in order to have peace and quiet, or to allow them to watch a noisy kids' TV show while I'm trying to cook/work/entertain/relax. So for those of you blessed with little 'uns, I totally understand you might want different rooms for different functions – open plan doesn't necessarily work for everyone.

There's also the matter of furnishing open-plan spaces … take away all the walls and where to put 'stuff' can be a challenge (though it's one I relish, and zoning spaces cleverly with furniture is lots of fun – see the box opposite for tips on this), as can placing kitchen units, radiators, TVs, and all the other bits and pieces we usually need a wall for.

But, in my mind, the benefits of having a space that is open are huge. Firstly, and obviously, your space feels much bigger, and you can enjoy more of it all at the same time. It's wonderfully sociable (I'll let you decide whether that's a positive or not!) and, for me, it means I'm only heating one space (albeit a larger one) which, given I almost exclusively use the wood burners for warmth, means lighting one fire, using

less fuel and generating less mess.

With an open-plan space you also often benefit from light running through the area from multiple directions. In the case of Admirals, given the kitchen is at the rear and is north-facing, then were the doors shut all the time, for half of the year the room would never get any direct sunlight. It would feel cold and uninviting and would require having the lights on nearly all the time. Conversely, the three huge, south-facing sash windows in the living room would be wasted if you're in the kitchen during the day. With the doors open, the sunlight streams through the whole space, especially in the winter when the sun is low in the sky, casting long shadows. In the summer, when the sun does make its way around the back, setting through the kitchen windows, the living room benefits from the glow and warmth. This alone is enough of a reason to create open or 'broken' spaces.

In Admirals, the doors are so wide that if you want any furniture in the living room, it's impossible to close them – not so much an issue for the Georgians who were fairly sparse with their furnishings, and used to keep it around the perimeter of the room until such time it was needed, but that's definitely not the way I like to live, so they shall remain permanently open.

How to create ZONES within a space

This is far from an exhaustive list, but there are lots of ways you can create zones within a large open-plan space that give the areas a defined look and use, rather than just having pieces of furniture floating about.

The first thing to think about is seating. Quite often, I see pieces of furniture too far apart from one another, especially in a large space. It doesn't matter what size your room is, if you want to have a pleasant conversation with someone, you can't sit 6 metres from them, so grouping furniture in a sociable distance is the first bit. Then, to ground it, you can add a rug – ideally large enough to get at least the front legs of all the furniture on it (with rugs generally it's a case of the bigger the better). Add a coffee table or ottoman in the centre and it's starting to look like its own zone.

Lighting also plays a huge part in zoning. You can bring a pendant light over that space, like I've done over the little kitchen table to help it feel more permanent, or, if this isn't possible, lamps can be placed on a table or wall. (There are even designs such as Castiglioni's Arco lamp that sit on the floor and can hang low over a coffee table – I had one in my last home.) At Admirals I've added a console table with lamps on behind the main sofa that really helps create that 'zone' around the fireplace and, when it's dark, being able to lighten and dim the different spaces, depending on what you're doing, really creates the feeling of intimacy and cosiness within a specific smaller space in a larger room.

You can use other furniture to zone spaces too – console tables or bookcases/shelving work well for this. You can also use colour or paint: the different coloured wallpapers in the same print I've used between the kitchen and living room do this, but adding a block of colour in a corner would also help define a space as a separate reading nook, for example.

The
LIVING
ROOM

THE

GROUND

FLOOR

Through the double doors from the kitchen is the living room. This space was in a similar state to the former dining room: rot, dirt and damage, and the radiators were even more interestingly placed – they'd been installed too near to the wall to fit a thermostatic valve on them, and one of the previous owner's solutions was to simply bash a hole in the lath and plaster to make space! There were ghastly modern inserts in the fireplaces that were totally inappropriate for the space and a carpet far older than I am that had sort of rotted and fused to the floorboards. The cornice needed some repairs and a modern picture rail taken away that did the room's proportions no favours whatsoever. The big double doors didn't really work properly and caught on the carpet … there were layers upon layers of wallpaper to remove and the windows had plywood pelmets that had damaged the architrave – not to mention some dubious electrics with sockets stuck randomly over some of the beautiful features. But, despite all this, with three huge south-facing windows the light is extraordinary and I could immediately see the room's potential.

The Layout

CREATING A COSY
SPACE WITHIN A
GRAND ROOM

W hilst quite a large room – 23 by 16 feet (7 by 4.9 metres) – as with lots of the rooms here at Admirals, the volume of architectural features (three windows to the front, the massive double doors opposite, a door in the centre of the back wall through to the hall with two alcoves either side of it, another to the rear hall and a large fireplace) makes it quite a challenging room to design in terms of layout.

As I mentioned earlier, I'm not a fan of sitting areas that are too spread out – it might be that years of drumming, motorcycling and using power tools has left me somewhat hard of hearing, but there's nothing worse than trying to have a conversation with someone seated far away. The same applies for the TV (unless you go for a huge screen, which then tends to dominate the room unless cleverly designed/hidden or embraced like in a cinema/media room – see page 103 for more on the placement of TVs) or fireplace when it's cold.

I therefore created a cosy sitting area by the fire, and effectively divided the room in two by placing the main sofa across the middle of the room, with a Georgian dresser base behind it (an excellent spot for lamps and drinks). Behind, there's another sitting area and a space that sort of welcomes you into the room. The partial barrier created by the lamps and dresser creates intrigue, giving a partial view through to the room, drawing the eye in with glimpses rather than revealing itself all in one go, while creating a natural route through the space and adding some useful storage.

Decorating

As mentioned in the last chapter, I wanted this space to feel harmonious with the kitchen, but not the same as it. It's a very bright room during the day, but I also wanted it to feel cosy and intimate in the evenings with the fire lit, so I used the same wallpaper print from Warner House (see page 90), but this time in a charcoal colourway, which, once on the walls, actually reads (to me at least, with my slightly dodgy eyes) as a rich, deep brown as the print has muted tones of pink, terracotta and taupe (I think – have I mentioned yet that I'm colour-blind?). Given the previously-mentioned architecture, there's not all that much in the way of walls, so it doesn't dominate, but it has a wonderfully soothing feeling while adding just a touch of drama to the space. The dark walls are also a

brilliant backdrop to art and the fabric for the curtains and upholstery, as well as the pale woodwork of the panelling and architrave contrasting beautifully against it. Again, the small pattern gives loads of texture and depth and it works so, so well.

Adding a large, neutral rug made from wool and sisal, sized specifically for the space and leaving just 30 centimetres of the oak floor visible, made things feel even cosier, while also absorbing sound and boosting the acoustics (and helping stop transmission of noise between the ground and lower ground floors). This type of textured, large rug is perfect for layering additional rugs over the top, with an old, hand-knotted Persian in front of the fire that adds warmth and pattern. (Old rugs are one

of my favourite things to add to a room – nearly every room has one and they add instant age and character to a space, especially when they're a little bit knackered and threadbare in places. There's something about them – having taken potentially months to make by hand with incredible skill, decades previously – that is so special.)

My ma and I made little café curtains for the windows, hung on solid brass rods. They add another bit of softness to the room, and a little privacy while still letting light filter in. It might look a little odd at first glance, but, as you can see, I haven't hung them equidistant between the curtain rail and the floor as about 5,000 people on Instagram insisted I must. The room is so tall that the rail is well over 6 feet (1.8 metres) from the

floor internally so, in doing so, the view would have been entirely obscured. The ground level outside the house is lower than inside, so by putting them where I did, no one can see in over them from the outside, but, when standing, you can see out.

These layer beautifully with the heavy, floor-to-ceiling drapes in another Persian-inspired print, this time taken from an early nineteenth-century shawl, which picks up on some of the colours in the wallpaper. The sinuous plants weave their way up the linen, drawing the eye upwards and making the most of the height of the room. They're also incredibly heavy and are interlined, brilliant for keeping things warm on an evening and keeping the draughts at bay from the sash windows.

Lighting

Once again, getting the lighting right in here was important. In a large space like this, you can't have something too small as the main, central light, especially given the ceiling roses are about 4 feet (1.2 metres) in diameter. (The ceiling roses in Admirals were truly functional, with gaps in the plasterwork, connected to pipework that ran in the void above to the exterior wall of the house and out through vents, to allow smoke and fumes from either candles or gas/paraffin lamps to escape – a bit of Georgian genius at work that's both beautiful and functional). Equally, I didn't want

something that dominated the space or blocked the light coming in from the windows and from travelling through the doors into the kitchen when the sun was out. An elegant, simple halo from Pooky with hand-painted shades works beautifully, and is accompanied by wall lights beside the over-mantel mirror, as well as library wall lights in the alcoves at the opposite side, as well as lots of lamps, all on smart dimmers again so it's effortless to turn them on and off. Pleated shades diffuse the light perfectly and are a brilliant opportunity to add pattern and colour.

A *NOTE* ON TELEVISONS

When thinking about the placement of the TV in your living room, there are a few things to consider. Personally, I'm not usually a fan of mounting them over fireplaces, for a number of reasons. Firstly, the aesthetic: a fireplace, to me, should be the main focal point in a space. By plonking a TV directly above it, you're pretty well making the TV the focal point, which isn't my preference, unless it's in a specific media or cinema room, but let's assume we're talking about a normal, multi-use living room at this point. (Though, in my last house, I did build a dedicated cinema room – but, even there, I put a second-hand motorised projector screen inside some wall-mounted cabinets. When it was off, it was completely hidden, with art on the walls, so there was very little evidence of a huge, 8-foot (2.4-metre) screen in the room.)

Secondly, while there are now many ways to hide a TV (which gets around my first objection), unless you've a very low fire, possibly without a surround or mantel, it puts the TV far higher than I find comfortable, and would likely lead to neck ache for those of us not used to donning Lycra and practising yoga. A TV, ideally, should be placed at a height that allows you to view it comfortably, with a level head, when you're sitting on the sofa, with your eyes somewhere in the middle(ish) of the screen. The further back from the TV you go, the less of an issue this is, but it's the equivalent of sitting in the front row of a cinema versus further back: one you're craning your neck to see anything, while the other is comfy.

So, where possible, in rooms with fireplaces, I choose to have the TV in an alcove. This might mean you need to turn your head slightly to see it, and causes a little compromise in speaker positioning and so on (I use a soundbar under the TV, with a hidden subwoofer under the dresser behind the sofa for some additional oomph), but this allows a natural height for the screen, as well as letting the fireplace sing – particularly with a mirror or art placed above it.

In the living room I've used a TV that can also display art which works remarkably well at disguising itself most of the time. A dark wall always helps when adding a TV too as they're usually dark in colour, and modern TVs are largely frameless, so a dark wall really disguises it. The walls in my last house were a deep indigo-navy blue, and the TV was placed against it – not disguised or covered – but because it blended so well into the wall, it certainly didn't draw attention to itself and was no competition for the huge fireplace in terms of what drew the eye.

Furniture

I generally love second-hand furniture. The sideboard behind the sofa is older than the house and gives an aged, lived-in feel. I've included a whole section on this (see page 226), but, when it comes to upholstery, I struggle to find good old pieces. It's possible, but harder than looking at things without upholstered elements. Partly, it's because, we (and I certainly) have gotten bigger, and heavier, over the last 200 years. Sitting in a Georgian, Victorian or Edwardian chair to me usually feels uncomfortable at best, and downright perilous at worst (usually for the chair, rather than me). They're often not designed for someone with my, erm, 'robust build', and 200 years of wear, despite them often being beautifully made, usually hasn't done much for their structural integrity. It's different for an occasionally used bedroom chair or one in the corner of the bathroom (both more likely to be used as a clothes horse than as an actual chair), in which case something small, old and pretty is often just the ticket. But for your main living space, that might often be crowded with people or have children bouncing all over it, or indeed might occasionally be used as a day bed for when the previous night's overindulgence requires a little R&R, new might be the way to go. Of course, new can still be made traditionally and built to last, and echo the shape and proportions of classic furniture, just built to fit a modern derriere!

Despite my love of second-hand, for the living room, lots of the furniture is new, for the reasons I mentioned above. For the main sitting area by the fire, I've chosen upholstered furniture that, while complementary, doesn't match – with different styles and fabrics. It really does feel like the furniture has been curated, collected and lived with... the sort of place you want to kick your shoes off and relax properly – not too stuffy or formal, which is how I like things generally, despite living in quite a grand, formal house.

In the other little zone I've created, on the other side of the dresser behind the sofa, for example, there's a pair of 1930s club chairs I picked up from an antiques shop in Plymouth. They're incredibly low and loungey and perfect for sitting with a cocktail and a book. As they're not all that frequently used (but look pretty), they can afford to be a little less robust than the new pieces. The leather and age of them provide wonderful contrast and another texture in the room and make something of an otherwise fairly dead space.

Colour, pattern and things not matching
definitely help add a relaxed air, as
does a mixture of old and new.

LIGHTING

The biggest thing to remember when lighting most rooms is to have everything on dimmer.

This is such an important thing to get right in a room as it can single-handedly make or break a space. Indeed, I'd go so far as to say that a very average room can become something really beautiful with the right lighting, especially as the evening begins to draw in.

Now, my experience is really limited to old houses – there's lots you can do with modern architecture and buildings, hiding LED strips everywhere that do all sorts of clever things and light paths and stairs and cornice and all that jazz, and it's grand in those sorts of buildings, but really isn't my cup of tea when it comes to lighting period properties (as well as being potentially difficult and invasive to fit).

I've also mentioned that I'm not a huge fan of masses of spotlights either. They definitely have their uses depending on the space, when they're used with thought and restraint, but they do seem to be the starting point for so many developers and similar when it comes to lighting a space.

The biggest things to remember when lighting most rooms is to have everything on dimmers – that's ceiling and wall lights, as well as all your lamps too, and to use warm LED bulbs in all sources.

You'll also likely need more lights than you might think – for example, in my bedroom, there are four lamps, two double wall sconces and the large main pendant globe, and this feels a bit 'light' in my opinion (excuse the pun!) to light the space adequately while having enough options to

create the mood I want. I'm very happy with the lighting in my living room and kitchen, though. The living room has five lamps, four wall lights and a main pendant, and the kitchen six wall lights, two pendants to zone the spaces, two four-track spotlights and the lights in the cooker hood and within the cupboards. It sounds like a lot, but this is what helps to create soft, gentle pools of light causing intrigue, casting shadows and creating zones – and with the help of dimmers, it lets you really play with the mood and feel of a space.

Generally speaking, I don't love being able to see the bulb itself. There are exceptions: lantern-style lighting, when used either very dimmed or sparingly as a secondary light source – as say the main pendant (only really turned on when looking for things, passing through or working/cleaning) – is fine, but I find that the bright glare of a visible bulb, unless dimmed almost to the point it's pretty well doing naught but decoration, throws off the balance of a space, is too harsh and often draws the eye too pointedly, blinding you to anything else in the room.

Diffused light, whether through fabric, frosted glass, ceramic, rattan or any other means, or a directional light, like an anglepoise, where the light source itself is pointed well away from the eyes, in my opinion creates a much softer and more agreeable ambience. There's also something incredibly beautiful about the way surfaces change as you flick the lights on – lamps becoming sculptural, pattern and colours leaping

out of fabrics; it really can create magic in a room.

Main lights are brilliant when you've got high ceilings to create drama and decoration, for drawing your eye upwards, creating a statement and adding colour or a little glamour and grandeur. They're also useful for when you need a bright light to 'do stuff', like find the TV remote that's been missing for a week. They're also very useful for creating zones in a room with more than one purpose, as I've mentioned already (see page 93). Often, however, they're rather poor at creating an attractive ambience, unless dimmed to a very gentle glow indeed. Again, there are exceptions. I've a light hanging above the little dining table in my kitchen. It obviously helps define that space as the area for the dining table as a 'zone'. I've got it hanging just above head height when seated and it's made from a carved-

out piece of solid alabaster. When lit, the light glows through the stone, casting warm light directly over the table. It's glorious and creates huge atmosphere when the rest of the room is dimmed, lighting the table gently, but throwing light up to the ceiling too which adds drama and interest. However, be careful how you use them and make sure that generally spaces can be lit adequately without the main light on.

Lamps, whether floor or table, are very much your friend here. They're an easy, affordable way to add massive impact to a room, usually requiring no electrics or messing about, even if you have to get a bit creative with wiring. The hamper under the dresser in the living room currently houses an extension cable for the lamps, while hiding a subwoofer I certainly wouldn't want on show (but thoroughly appreciate when watching a movie),

but one day I'll get round to routing the wires properly up the back leg of the dresser and into one of the drawers so they seamlessly disappear.

You can probably also see from my photos that I'm a huge fan of pleated fabric shades. Even when the lamp is turned off, they add so much pattern and colour to a room, and, when lit, they're beautiful. Fabric shades are also timeless and work well in a huge range of interiors, from a workers' cottage to a palace. They're so easy to change and replace, and I quite like moving lamps around the house to change the look of a space. With large rooms, getting lamps into the middle of a space again makes a massive difference to the feel of a space and is useful for reading too.

With my lamps, I generally use Philips Hue bulbs. They feel like a bit of an investment as they aren't cheap, but being able to turn on all the lamps, change the brightness of them all and turn them back off again effortlessly, from my phone or even using voice commands, is just brilliant (and I've yet to have a guest who doesn't love it when I tell Alexa to 'dim living room lights' to see all the lamps in the room dim automatically). The thought of having to go around the room turning lamps on and off constantly and then fettling individually with the settings for each one endlessly throughout the night, well, I likely wouldn't bother – whereas in my living room, I am constantly tweaking as the evening and use of the room changes, which massively enhances the feel of the space. I've the same, for example, with all my hardwired kitchen and living room lighting, but this is done through smart switches rather than in the bulb, which means I can use far cheaper bulbs.

Bathrooms can be a bit trickier. I'm lucky to have good-sized bathrooms with a lot of ceiling height, so I can have pendant lighting. I often think bathrooms are too harshly lit, so, once again, I have all lighting on dimmers. Where you're lighting a sink, two lights – one either side of the mirror – gives a more flattering light than one overhead light, lighting the face evenly and not casting any shadows. In a bathroom, wall lights generally are your friend and you can now buy cost-effective IP44 rated wall lights from the likes of Pooky, suitable for bathroom use, that can be paired with fabric or paper shades to give a much softer, warmer and more flattering light than a sea of overhead spotlights, while also adding colour, pattern and character.

Kitchens are similar to bathrooms. I've already talked about this in the kitchen chapter, but, again, I would, if you can, resist the temptation to put in a huge grid of spotlights. By all means use them where necessary, in a considered way, but introduce other light sources, just as you would in any other room. Yes, you need things to be light and bright when prepping and cooking food, but assuming your kitchen is for more than just cooking in, being able to light it softly, warmly and elegantly, in a flattering way for the room and occupants, makes an enormous difference to how you can actually use the space.

I've only started a little on the outside lighting at Admirals – it's something I'm really looking forward to learning more about – but the vaults and area leading down to the lower ground has been relit. I tried to replicate a similar feel to the lighting I already found down there (very old, knackered and alas beyond saving) that definitely had a bit of a nod to the nautical. Indeed, it may well have been items used on boats and certainly in the dockyard, being naval-owned, with caged bulkhead lighting. A mixture of lighting types, all in beautiful, solid cast brass from the Soho Lighting Company, made in the UK, are just perfect for this application. With solid stone walls, there's no way of hiding the wires, and previously they'd used steel conduit that had inevitably turned to rust outside and crumbled when you touched it, so we redid it in copper and brass fittings. Originally designed for plumbing, they work beautifully in a slightly more workman-like space, like the entrance to the servants' quarters, and will soften and age beautifully as they patinate over time. And, unlike steel, they will last almost indefinitely.

The SMALLEST ROOM
(in the house)

THE

GROUND

FLOOR

Gosh, this one was a real charmer when I moved in – a wire coat hanger stopped the plastic toilet cistern from leaking (just), it had a window that didn't close properly, dead mice were hidden beneath the flooring, and the ceiling, made of hardboard, had, for no discernible reason, been lowered by 4 feet (1.2 metres). Generally, it was just all very, very grim, but very satisfying to tackle.

When *you* can't look *out*, look up

GRANDEUR IN THE
SMALLEST SPACES

First, I, very satisfyingly, took a hammer to the weird, dropped ceiling and was thrilled to find a 3-foot (90-centimetre) void above it, albeit with some now-redundant pipework that needed removing. When the space is so small (about 3 by 4 feet/0.9 by 1.2 metres), any extra volume, even directly above your head, was definitely going to help make it feel a little grander and less claustrophobic.

I properly wracked my brain and exhausted all options with trying to fit a sink in here, and in the end I just couldn't do it (without it being a sort of basin-over-lavatory-type thing, like you might find on an aeroplane, that I wouldn't have been able to even fit my hand in, or putting it to one side that would have meant using the facilities at an angle – and likely banging your head on it when standing back up!). Eventually, when I come to do the space, I've decided that the back hallway that the WC is off will have a sort of vintage-looking ceramic bowl and jug combo (all plumbed in) set atop an antique dresser or similar, for hand-washing purposes.

Of all the spaces in your home, should your heart desire it, I think the downstairs loo is the place where you can go wildest with the decor. Not only does no one (hopefully, short of any kitchen disasters) spend too long in there, so if they absolutely hate it, that's OK, it's also a place lots of guests are likely to see, so a big old lump of 'wow' factor, even if it's a bit divisive, is no bad thing – it makes for an excellent conversation-starter if nothing else! Given the nature of its usage, no one needs to take themselves too seriously in there, so it's somewhere you can have a bit of fun as well.

Obviously, I want the WC to flow well enough from the spaces leading to it, but, in this instance, I chose a bold, exotic wallpaper from Warner House based on the pictorial Chamba Rumal from the eighteenth century, and have used a Georgian-style wide, bead and butt panelling on the lower section of the walls, painted in a mid-green eggshell.

The small-scale mosaic design helps in a tiny space and I deliberately chose a pattern that had a square border, to throw the eye and really show how much of an odd space the room is.

I love panelling like this in bathrooms. It protects the walls, is scrubbable, can be easily repainted if necessary through damage (or if you fancy redecorating), is generally far cheaper than nice tiles and feels a little warmer to the touch too, not a small consideration in a place you're likely to be semi-naked with walls as close together as this. It's still bloomin' cold in here though so, to help take some of the nip out of the air, I've installed electric underfloor heating (the room being too small to sensibly install a radiator), but as that part of the house is yet to be rewired, it's not been connected yet.

On the floor I chose a small-scale mosaic design. The small scale helps in a tiny space and I deliberately chose a pattern that had a square boarder, to throw the eye and really show how much of an odd space the room is ... again, a bit of fun in a space that isn't taking itself too seriously!

The star of the show here, though, is the glorious privy itself. Not only do high-level cisterns look great in an old house like this, they're also space-saving too. By mounting the bulk of the cistern way up high, the actual pan sits closer to the wall, jutting out less into the room – very useful in this instance. It also draws the eye up, again giving a greater sense of space, and, in my last house, faced with a similarly tiny WC with a very awkwardly placed window, I actually took the cistern up and around a corner to be on an adjacent wall – sounds weird, but it worked a treat.

Add a throne-like seat and a crystal chandelier (this was up in the hallway when I bought the house, so covered in dust it was unrecognisable, so I stripped it all down, rewired it, put all the crystal into the dishwasher and it came out gleaming) and, all together, it's turned a very grim space into something with a little faded grandeur that makes most people smile (and perhaps one or two wince, but that's OK).

PREP WORK

The biggest task in most of Admirals' rooms has been the paint-stripping and woodwork prep, with months of scraping, washing, sanding and filling before the fun bits can happen. Prep is everyone's least favourite job (and anyone who tells you that they 'like' sanding is lying, or just hasn't done enough of it to know the truth!).

If you follow me on Instagram, you might have seen just how much of my life is given to preparation, particularly of the woodwork. There's a lot of it here, and the paintwork is often cracking, blistering and peeling off, as well as obliterating all the details in the woodwork.

I've painstakingly removed the paint from all the woodwork as I've been going through the house. The good news is that, if your paintwork is in good condition, this is unnecessary, but, in some circumstances, it's unavoidable – and you have my sympathy. It's a dangerous exercise in an old house too thanks to the aforementioned lead-based paint you're almost certain to have, but after finding myself poisoned from the stuff, I did then start using Kling Strip paint remover, an alkaline poultice stripper which is thankfully much, much safer to use (so long as you don't get it on your skin … it burns, as I found out with a shock when I hoisted up my trousers with my thumbs in the back of the waistband. I had some Kling Strip on my gloves, which went down the back of my trousers and, well, a few minutes later I was sprinting to the bath and was the proud owner of a couple of blisters on my backside!). Despite this minor blip, it has been, quite literally, a lifesaver.

Stripping everything back is still a massive amount of work though – the paint remover is incredibly heavy, at 30 kilograms for a 15-litre tub, and, given the areas I have to do, takes significant effort to put on (you'll hurt in places you didn't realise you had muscles after a day of it). I use a plasterer's trowel to put it on and it needs to go on thick enough (in my case, about 2.5 centimetres), before you leave it (again, in my case, about 48 hours), before then scraping it all off, hopefully taking all the paint with it until you're back to bare wood.

At that point the clear up begins. This is the longest part of the job, as if you don't clean and scrape thoroughly, then the alkaline will remain in the wood and cause your new paint to peel off – not ideal! So, lots of scrubbing and washing with water, more scraping to get it all out of the detail and yet more scrubbing, over and again, is needed until the water runs clear. At that stage you need to go over it with a neutraliser to bring the pH back down to normal and then let it dry. And the cycle of sanding and filling and sanding and more filling and cleaning and caulking and knotting and priming and caulking and more sanding can begin.

Prep really is tedious work. However, it is so important if you're hoping to achieve a finish that's not only strokably smooth and good to look at, but also one that's going to last, rather than just end up chipping and cracking and peeling away in months. Sadly, I've learned this the hard way. The first bedroom I did (mine), I prepped the same way I did my first house, thoroughly sanding and filling but not removing the paint. Alas, the woodwork is

Prep really is tedious work. However, it is so important if you're hoping to achieve a finish that's not only strokably smooth and good to look at, but also one that's going to last.

already cracking and has all sorts of issues.

Speaking of sanding, something I wish I'd done much sooner, after the lead poisoning debacle, was to invest in a proper dust extractor and matching sander, both by Festool. They feel unfathomably expensive for what they are, but they work so effectively. Combined with their own paper (again, it's not worth skimping on), they work quickly and with very little dust. I then use their backing sponge pads to allow me to sand curves, and even cut them down and build them up, allowing me to use the machine on areas that would otherwise be inaccessible.

After that, using a tack cloth to get the surfaces clean before knotting and priming really helps give a good finish, as does a very light de-nib sanding after priming and possibly your first coat too.

This isn't intended as a tutorial; it's just a few tips I've picked up. The internet and places like Instagram and YouTube are awash with tutorials from people far more knowledgeable than I am, but I'm often doing little videos or write-ups on my Instagram page that might be useful.

The
FIRST
FLOOR

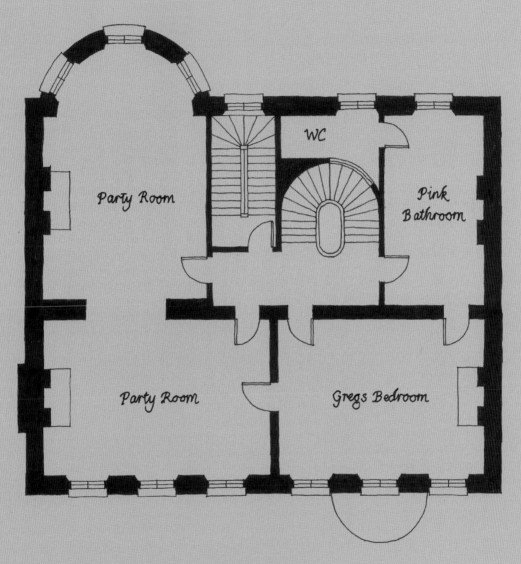

Party Room

WC

Pink
Bathroom

Party Room

Gregs Bedroom

First Floor Plan

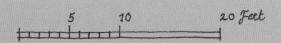

5   10   20 Feet

The MAIN BEDROOM

THE

FIRST

FLOOR

One of the first spaces I tackled in the main house – there's nothing like having a comfortable, clean bedroom to retreat to after a hard day grafting. It's been a much needed sanctuary over the last few years and I live in it as much as I did when I'd first completed it.

The Grandest Bedroom in the House

FIT FOR AN ADMIRAL

It's hard to know if there ever were once bedrooms on this floor – certainly there would never have been bathrooms given the house pre-dates indoor plumbing. The Georgians, in tall town houses such as this, often used the first floor as formal rooms as well as the ground floor, with a parlour and dining room downstairs, and the drawing rooms on the first, hence the first floor retaining almost identical proportions and features as the ground floor in terms of cornice, fine woodwork, shutters, fireplaces, and so on, with the only real difference being a slightly reduced ceiling height of 10.5 feet (3.2 metres) versus 11.5 (3.5 metres).

The main bedroom is actually the only bedroom on this floor, and is attached to a bathroom with Jack and Jill doors, so there's a door from the bedroom, but also one into the hall. The room sits directly on top of the elliptical entrance hall, and shows just how much space is wasted by those lovely curved walls, occupying the same footprint but feeling cavernous in comparison. Being the grandest of all the bedrooms, it is, of course, the one I've chosen for myself ... it also saves the legs from an extra flight of stairs come bedtime, and means, when I do have guests to stay, they're on the floor above and everyone is afforded a bit of space and privacy.

Decor

With three south-facing windows to the front, high ceilings and being far wider across the front than it is deep, this is a very light, bright room so my starting point in here was the colour. I chose to take the same rich, deep blue ('Burnham Overy' by Fenwick & Tilbrook) across all the walls, woodwork and cornice, with a soft, muted putty on the ceiling. It makes a big space feel instantly cosier, calmer and, dare I say it, a little bit sexy too. It also provides the perfect backdrop for art, furniture and that beautiful, original Carrara marble fireplace that horrifyingly was covered in many, many layers of paint and needed stripping back. I know I've said it before, but everything just looks better against a dark background.

Painting nearly everything in one colour (also known as Colour Drenching) has a harmonious effect on a room. Without lots of lines and changes to draw the eye and define the boundaries of the space, it really does bring a quietness despite the dramatic colour.

Over the bed hangs a tapestry that gives some softness and is a relatively inexpensive way of adding massive statement artwork, and at the windows, are heavy velvet curtains in a print taken from another eighteenth-century hand-painted chinoiserie, this time found at Hurst Park, near Horsham. The background colour is nearly a perfect match to the walls, again adding harmony, and, all in all, it feels very luxurious.

It's hard to imagine anyone ever thinking that slapping paint on a marble fireplace surround was a good idea.

BEAUTIFUL – BUT
NOT VERY COSY!

Flooring

I had intended to restore the floorboards in here, but with Georgian boards, they're straight cut at the side, rather than tongue-and-groove boards as you'd find in the Victorian period and onwards. This makes them very noisy and draughty, unless all those gaps are appropriately filled with slivers of wood or similar. They also weren't in great condition and I was keen to try to easily add a little sound and heat insulation, so I chose a fine sisal weave carpet – another natural product and something that feels appropriate in nearly any setting, whether old or new. It gives a similar feel in terms of texture and interest to a wooden floor, but, when combined with its underlay, adds significantly more warmth and 'hush' to a room, helping the acoustics. It's also perfect to layer over, and I've added yet another Persian rug underneath the bed adding further warmth, colour, pattern and comfort. It smells wonderful too.

One of the few jobs I don't tackle myself is the laying of carpets. The rooms at Admirals are so big, and there are endless opportunities for me to get it horribly wrong, that it's just not worth the risk. You need some quite specific tools, especially when the carpets need joining or you're dealing with sisal, and, to me, it's a job worth paying a professional to do. I also don't take on my own plastering. I've tried it, and am absolutely hopeless at it. It takes me ten times longer to get half as good a finish and I make an almighty mess! It's the sort of job I think you need to do a lot of to really get the feel of it, but, in my mind, if you can find a good plasterer (and fortunately I have – thanks, Wayne!), it's worth letting them crack on once you've done as much prep work for them as you can.

Furniture

With three doors, three windows and a fireplace, this is another room that's really difficult to actually do too much with and, as with some of the other spaces, where the nasty tin radiators had been added meant even fewer places to add any furniture. I moved the radiators into the windows, which now house traditional, free-standing cast-iron beauties, which freed up a couple of spots for chests of drawers. I've added antique pieces, found mainly through Facebook Marketplace and auction houses for pennies, and a timeless hardwood and cane sleigh bed.

There's nowhere to put a wardrobe in here without either blocking a door or obscuring a window, which I wasn't keen to do. (It's worth remembering that Georgians, even quite wealthy ones like the original Admiral, wouldn't have had all that much in the way of 'stuff' like clothes and so on, and what they did have would have been kept somewhere by the household staff, ready to bring as required, so the notion of storage as we see it today would be somewhat lost on them.) I therefore don't keep much in the way of clothing in here (as you'll come to see further on in the book), which is occasionally a bit of a faff, but it does mean I'm able to keep it tidier, in theory at least, and, again, helps with the calming theme, making it a grand place to doze off for the night.

Finishing Touches

I opened the fireplace back up, removing the modern monstrosity, and stripped away the magnolia paint all over the marble surround. It isn't functional, but at least it looks the part now. I've added a Georgian mirror over it and, while I think the room still needs some finishing touches, it's not far off.

Above a console table, I've also chosen to hang a piece of colourful art I commissioned a friend of mine, Tom Glendenning, to paint – his first after leaving art college – and it is a treasured possession. It used to sit in my old kitchen, against walls that were a very similar colour, and it works really well in here, nicely balancing the older oil painting and chinoiserie and stopping everything feeling too old and stuffy.

ONE OF THE FEW THINGS I TOOK WITH ME FROM MY LAST HOME, THIS PIECE PAINTED BY GOOD FRIEND TOM GLENDENNING

PAINTING

In terms of which bits to paint in a room, picture rails seem to be where lots of people (myself included) trip up a bit. My last place had picture rails and I did what most do – paint up to the picture rail in the colour of the wall and above it in the same colour as the ceiling. In most cases, this has the negative effect of visually lowering your ceiling height; essentially your eyes get to the picture rail and then, because everything above is the ceiling colour, they assume that's where it starts. Obviously, the difference is more marked when there's a strongly contrasting colour, but taking the paint colour up and over the picture rail makes a huge difference in how the space feels. Similarly, if you're wallpapering, take the paper above the picture rail too. Either way, if you're doing this, I would paint the picture rail in either the same colour as the wall or the best match you can find to the wallpaper's background colour (in either instance, use an eggshell paint for wood rather than the wall paint, for durability). Ultimately, the picture rail needs to sit as quietly as possible on the wall, drawing as little attention to itself as it can.

The cornice is a little more up for grabs. If wallpapering, I would simply paint the cornice the same colour as the ceiling, and this is a fairly classic way to do things. However, in my bedroom for example, the ceilings, while high, seem slightly low for the proportion of the rest of the room, so I've taken the wall colour up and onto the cornice. Similarly with going above the picture rail (which I've also done in this space), this again adds visual height to the ceiling. It also adds a bit of drama too, so is definitely something to consider.

And when it comes to ceilings, they don't have to be white (but it's OK if that's the way you want to go – it's classic and works well almost everywhere). If you do choose to go for white, I would say don't go for a brilliant or 'pure' white. It's usually a very cold colour and, unless under very forgiving light, can come off as a bit bluey-grey. I don't think pure white has a place in an old house at all if I'm honest – it feels to me utterly joyless and far too sterile! For my 'white' I use Fenwick & Tilbrook's 'Dandelion'. Named after the smudgy white/soft grey seed heads of said delicious weed, it's a wonderfully forgiving, neutral shade. It's just got that touch of grey undertone to soften the white, toning things down, while being warm enough to work in cool light, but not so warm it reads as a cream or magnolia. It'll go with everything and feels very sympathetic to an old house.

On ceilings (or cornice or any other plasterwork you might have, like ceiling roses), you want the paint to be as flat/matt as possible. Rarely is old plasterwork free of imperfections and the same can be said for ceilings. I still use one that's washable, but very matt in finish. As always, there are exceptions to the rule though: a gloss ceiling in the right hands can look extraordinary, but the chance of a DIYer (and likely lots of professionals) getting a beautiful, smooth, mirror-like finish is slim and it would be a huge effort and take many, many days, or even weeks.

It's the same with wall paint – my preference is for a very matt, washable finish (Fenwick & Tilbrook's 'pure matt plus'). It feels most appropriate in these old buildings, goes on beautifully and hides any little imperfections there might be.

When it comes to woodwork, I used to be very much a fan of traditional, oil-based eggshell. Alas, this is something that's very hard to get hold of now and was always messy and difficult to use. It has all but been entirely replaced by water-

based finishes which have improved massively. I use Fenwick & Tilbrook's exterior eggshell (there's no harm in using the exterior paint internally like this), which comes in with around a 20 per cent sheen level (the paint of theirs I use on walls and ceilings is more like 3 per cent for comparison). They do an interior one too, but it's too matt for my personal taste at 10 per cent.

Again, most people paint all trim in the same white. As before, if you're going down this route, my preference is for something a lot softer and more muted than a pure white which feels harsh and modern to my eyes. I actually don't use a traditional 'white' at all, and have opted in a lot of rooms for a slightly darker, soft putty colour. It's still pale and will go with absolutely anything, but again feels far more sympathetic than a harsh

white. Having said that, I would question whether painting all the woodwork in the same colour is the right choice. It might be; it always feels classic and smart, but can also feel quite busy, especially when you're using lots of contrasting colours against it. In most rooms, I've either chosen a colour sympathetic to the other colours in the room or painted it the same colour as the walls. This gives a harmonious effect to the space and stops any straight lines shouting too loudly for attention, giving the effect of rooms appearing larger and calmer. Through the entrance hall and then into the living room and kitchen, spaces I very much see as being used together as one, I used the same soft, putty colour throughout that would go with all the wall coverings, helping the spaces to mesh together calmly.

The PINK BATHROOM

THE FIRST FLOOR

The bathroom adjoining the main bedroom, while a good size, with the same, tall ceilings, faces north, so gets much cooler light and really this was the starting point for the space. It's quite unusual in that the lavatory is in a separate room off the main bathroom – in a little space created behind the internal curve of the staircase wall, that then has a large (thankfully patterned and obscured) window, allowing light through on to the stairs. This means the main bathroom has three doors – again, not ideal when you're trying to fit a bathroom in a space and, given its listed status, it's not simply a case of being able to block up a door or similar (and they all serve a purpose!).

The Layout

I LIKE BATHROOMS TO BE
TREATED AND DECORATED
IN THE SAME WAY AS I
WOULD ANY OTHER ROOM
IN A HOME, SO THEY FEEL
COMFORTABLE AND
RELAXED AND NOT TOO
COLD AND STERILE.

This was the first bathroom in the main house I tackled and was in a very sorry state. With historic leaks, about twenty layers of wallpaper on the walls, all of which had been glossed over, some 'interesting' plywood built-in cupboards and holes in the walls from old pipes, it needed stripping right back to its bare bones to make any sense of it. The wallpaper in places was so stubborn it took the old plaster with it so there was a lot of remedial work needed too. Once that was done, I could start to focus.

In sorting the layout for this bathroom, I wanted a large, walk-in shower (I'm not a fan of doors or lots of moving parts in a shower – it makes them tricky to keep clean and they look heavier in the space). I prefer showers to be as invisible as possible in the room, and this pretty well dictated where it had to go, being the only corner of the room without anything in it. The bathtub went pride of place opposite the fireplace and then, opposite the doorway from the landing (so frequently seen), I've put the console-like basin.

It's important, where you have the option based on space and plumbing, that you consider what you see in a bathroom when the door is open, given they often are to allow light into the landings and to air the room too. Ideally, a lavatory is hidden away from view, or at least not the first thing your eyes are drawn to. Basins tend to work well where possible as there are many out there that feel more like furniture, especially if you add a pretty mirror and some lighting – it gives a really warm welcome into the space. In here I've chosen a basin made from jet-black porcelain – a bold choice, but one that also helps to trick the eye into it not feeling too much like a typical bathroom.

Decor

The sludgy, dirty pink on the walls really helps to warm up the space without it feeling too sugary sweet and, countered with a dark blue on some of the woodwork and bath, it grounds the space nicely. A timeless marble floor and whimsical wallpaper depicting drawings of trees from the late 1700s from the Natural History Museum, from Divine Savages, define the funny little curved room with the toilet in and round things off nicely. (Though, being the first time I ever tried wallpapering, this was not the best room to start with as it has lots of awkward, acute angles and curves. While I learned a lot, don't look too closely at the finish.)

A huge, mirrored, antique French armoire adds lots of useful storage and the sweet little chair my ma and I upholstered together adds softness, colour and pattern. It's very rare it's ever used, but, if you've space for it, I think a chair (or, even better, a chaise longue) in a bathroom exudes a feeling of luxury ... the fact it's not

often sat in doesn't really matter, it's more about what it suggests than is actually used for.

The fireplace was another that needed the paint removing and the whole thing restoring. Somewhat heartbreakingly, someone at some point had decided the fireplace would be a brilliant place to add a radiator, actually drilling into the marble itself to hang the brackets – madness and something I'm still yet to fix properly.

The main event once you're in the room though is the artwork above the bath. They are beautiful, chinoiserie-inspired paintings by the incredibly talented artist Diane Hill (who also created the print on the chair and its cushion) and make such a statement. They are so beautiful and really add to the whole vintage, comfortable feel of the space.

BATHS

A word on baths while I have you ... It may surprise you, given the number of baths I've already installed here, that I rarely have a bath and am definitely more of a shower man. However, where you've got the space, a free-standing bath is such a statement of luxury, I like to include them where I can.

A cast-iron roll top bath is a beautiful thing, but they're also very heavy and very cold, so I go for ones that are made from a sort of limestone resin. They're just as solid and strong feeling as cast iron, but quite a lot lighter and don't feel so cold. They'll also last almost indefinitely, being both super strong and with an internal finish that is very durable and can be easily refinished (it's actually not a 'finish' at all, but just the raw material that's polished smooth, so, unlike the enamel on a cast-iron bath, as robust as it is, there's no coating to chip or scratch and any wear can be polished out). It's a wonderful material. They aren't cheap when new, but I've bought most of mine second-hand from sites like eBay and similar for about £100, and then cleaned them up and painted the outside of them (they're very easy to paint in this material). They feel brand new once installed.

I would avoid, where possible, anything plastic or acrylic. They won't last as long, aren't repairable, flex, twist and creak (which can also then lead to leaks where they're sealed), look terrible if they get scratched or worn and, in the long run, will end up costing you more.

A cast-iron roll top bath is a beautiful thing, but they're also very heavy and very cold, so I go for ones that are made from a sort of limestone resin.

The
PARTY
ROOM

THE

FIRST

FLOOR

Directly above the double rooms that comprise the living room and kitchen-diner are what I refer to as the 'party room', certainly not being fancy enough to have two drawing rooms! Though nowhere near as large as the one downstairs, the opening between these spaces is a beautiful, panelled arch. Sadly, though, it is now missing its original door that must have been taken off many years ago.

An Unexpected Partnership

WHEN GLAMOUR
VISITED ADMIRALS

I'd intended to leave these rooms right until the end of the project, as, without a functioning kitchen and bathroom, it was unlikely I was going to be throwing any wild parties anytime soon (and the less said about COVID-19 and lockdowns the better!). However, fate had other plans and, before I'd even started doing any proper work on the house, the incredible print and pattern designer Anna Hayman got in touch. She'd absolutely fallen in love with the space and what I was doing with the house, having seen it on Instagram, and wondered if I might like us to work together to create something really special.

Well, it was too exciting to say no to, so we started hatching a bit of a plan. Given that these are spaces that aren't going to be frequently used, and are quite celebratory in nature, I was keen to push my boundaries a bit and go for something that was slightly away from my usual style – a little bit like visiting your favourite cocktail bar or restaurant – and Anna was perfect for this. An absolute whizz with pattern and colour, her whole style is gorgeous, elegant and sophisticated (therefore quite different from the author, dear reader). Albeit with a slightly more 'art deco'-inspired twist than my own tastes, Anna's flair taught me so much about using pattern in a space, which was the initial push I needed to give me the confidence to give it a whirl in other rooms too.

I got to work starting to restore the spaces. The biggest job in here, after the woodwork, was the floor, from which I painstakingly pulled what felt like a million staples and nails, hand-scraped all the Victorian-era bitumen from around the edges (the Victorians added this nasty stuff to darken the areas not covered by a rug, in an attempt to make pine floors look more like a hardwood – believe me, if you haven't had the joy of trying it yourself, it's horrible to remove), fixed all the boards down so they were nice and solid, and then hand-sanded everything until smooth. If I'd used a proper floor sander it would have been too aggressive and most of the character in the boards, which I was keen to keep, would have been taken away. By hand-sanding, the wear and patination in the floor remained.

There were also walls and ceilings to repair, fireplaces to restore with new hearths laid, and a full wire and replumb of the heating with new radiators all round. The rear fireplace was again very badly damaged and actually about to collapse off the wall, so I had to remove it completely to make good, repair it and reattach it safely – they're such big lumps of marble and very heavy, so are definitely not something you want falling unexpectedly off the wall!

Here, I installed a beautiful, traditionally styled wood-burning stove to help warm the space and, in the front fireplace, I removed the awful, modern insert and replaced it with a salvaged, original cast-iron example I found from the right era to the house on eBay. It needed a good going over, but came up beautifully.

LOTS OF SAMPLES WERE
NEEDED TO FIND THE
PERFECT SHADE!

While I was doing this, Anna was working on print designs and colours, hand-cutting lino to then block-print the ceiling wallpaper. We'd decided to put pattern on the ceiling, subtly referencing the ornate ceilings you'd find in a grand Georgian stately home, and Anna picked up references, like the Greek key you see above the picture rail, from the architecture around the hospital site (you can see this motif on the beautiful gate pillars on the entrance to 'the square' on page 18).

We created our own colour for the space with Fenwick & Tilbrook over in Norfolk that I was allowed to name – I went with 'Drunken Sailor' to reference the naval history of the site, and the intended use of the room! This green is reminiscent of the arsenic green so popular throughout the late Georgian and Victorian period. It wasn't known initially that it was poisonous in its use in paint, but as the popularity of the colour grew, so too did reports of arsenic poisoning which included rashes, headaches, stomach issues and, in the very worst cases, death. Even once its poisonous qualities were known, the appetite for the colour was so high that people continued to use it right through until 1880, at which point non-poisonous alternatives had been found.

Anna even worked with Dominic Schuster, an expert in such things, to create the two, incredible hand-aged mirrors in the same green. They're absolutely breathtaking in their texture and character.

Another element Anna worked on was the floor covering, alongside the incredible, local carpet-makers Axminster, who actually invented the way to make this type of carpet on a loom, the founder having been so impressed with the handwoven rugs he'd seen in Turkey. This was back in 1755, and they continue to make carpets in the same way today, still in Axminster. There's also a lovely connection to Saltram House, a grand Georgian stately home owned by the National Trust about 5 miles away from Admirals House, that is home to one of the most impressive Axminster rugs in the world. They've recently rewoven this carpet to create an exact replica as

it would have been and it's impossible to think that Captain Creyke wouldn't, at some point, have been at a grand event or party at Saltram and walked upon that very carpet. Anna and I had fallen in love with the marbled paper that you find lining the insides of old Victorian books, so they worked at turning it into a bespoke rug for the space.

Since completing this room, I've come to realise that any huge parties I have are likely to be centred around either the kitchen or the garden (again, the staff these grand houses would once have had would have made ferrying food and drink up and down stairs all

evening much easier – if only!). The front side of the party room still works beautifully as a sort of formal(ish) living room; bathed in sunlight it's just perfect. I've created a comfortable, but more formal seating arrangement around the fire using a pair of identical sofas. There's no TV in here, so the layout, facing each other, works really well for smaller gatherings.

But, reflecting on how I live, now working from home and spending more time at my desk (well, currently the kitchen table, but one day ...) than I'd ever expected to, I'm actually going to look to reinstate the doors between the two spaces and redecorate the rear room into a sort of 'gentleman's library' of sorts. Imagine lots of books and intriguing objects as if I'd just come back from my very own 'Grand Tour' as the wealthy young Georgian men might have once done – a place for me to work, with a huge old partners desk, worn wingback chairs by the fireplace and a well-stocked liquor cabinet. I'm actually going to create some kind of built-in home cinema-type thing that will be hidden when not used, but be a fun place to light the wood burner and watch movies one day.

A *NOTE* ON RESTORING CAST-IRON FIREPLACES

In a lot of the rooms here at Admirals, behind the boarded-up fireplaces, I was very lucky to find a selection of the original cast-iron inserts. They were in various states of disrepair, but I was grateful to have them all the same. The good news is, they're very forgiving and satisfying to restore to get them gleaming again (though, as I mentioned earlier, I don't use any of these open fireplaces due to their inefficiency. If you're looking at recommissioning a fireplace, I implore you to speak to an expert to get the fireplace and chimney looked at properly to check they're safe to light as there's an excellent chance they won't be without some work.

Lots of the cast-iron inserts I found were painted, often black, which I never really understood (if yours aren't then you can luckily skip this step), so the first job is to remove any paint. The good news is that, on cast iron, this is quite straightforward as Kling Strip (see page 116) does a beautiful job and is far quicker than when using it on wood as the metal doesn't absorb any of the water/product and it all cleans down beautifully. Once all the paint's removed, you can give it a good clean and start going over it with a wire brush to remove any remaining debris and, most importantly, any rust – I use ones attached to my drill which save a lot of effort.

At this point, everywhere should be back to gleaming metal. I give it all a wipe down with methylated spirit (don't use water or the rust will come back) and then go over it all with a layer of iron paste (I use the one from Liberon). It's very messy and I always forget to put on gloves, but, once gently buffed back, it protects the ironwork and gives it a gentle graphite-like sheen and stops it from rusting.

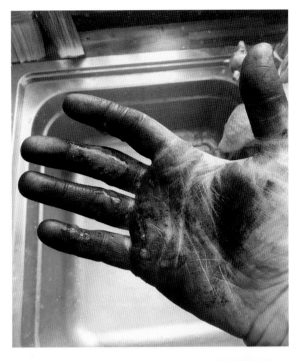

A GRUBBY JOB THAT
MAKES A HUGE
DIFFERENCE

The
SECOND
FLOOR

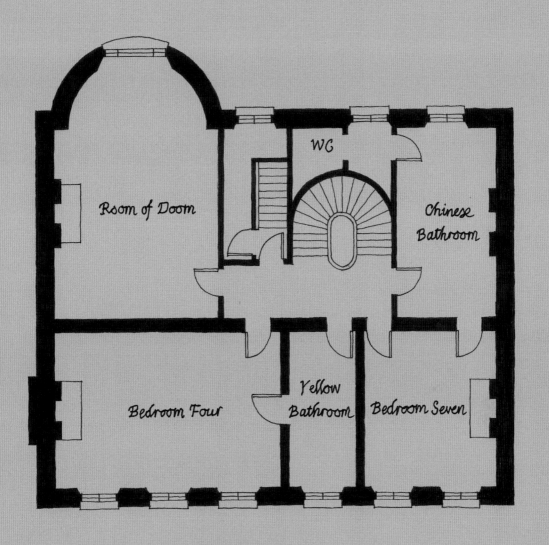

Room of Doom

WC

Chinese Bathroom

Bedroom Four

Yellow Bathroom

Bedroom Seven

Second Floor Plan

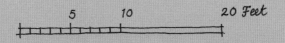

5   10   20 Feet

The
ROOM *of*
DOOM

THE

SECOND

FLOOR

I should probably call this something else now, as it no longer feels quite so doom-laden, but it was undoubtedly one of the worst rooms in the house when I viewed it. Alas, the name seems to have stuck, though it always raises an eyebrow if I've friends to stay and I tell them they're staying in the room of doom ...!

Back *to* Basics

AND KEEPING OUT
THE PIGEONS!

It was full of 'stuff', had pigeons living in the old cupboards, was freezing as the window was ajar and unable to close, and there was significant damage from leaks, some from water coming in from outside (from the same blocked gutter that had caused damage in the now kitchen) and some internal leaks that came from a cracked shower tray above, for which the solution was buckets placed on the servants' staircase (that were stagnant and overflowing when I viewed it for the first time).

It had also been painted in various metallic hues (dark blue glittery walls and a gunmetal glitter door), had CDs stuck to the walls and woodwork, and a large hole drilled into the door – with the only logical reason being to allow cats to come and go perhaps. There was also major damage to the ceiling and cornice. The room was so bad that the previous owners had boarded it up with a stud wall going halfway across the landing. We had to cut an arch through it so I could view it when I first looked round.

Let's just say, this room needed a bit of love showing to it!

Given the state the room was in, there was a lot to unpick here – loads of paint to strip from the walls and woodwork, loose or rotten plaster to remove, about thirty pigeons' nests and guano to take out and lots of the supporting timbers had pretty well turned to dust from the water ingress. Old lead pipes from a basin needed cutting out, obviously a whole rewire was required and the radiators needed repositioning and replacing with cast-iron units. Once this was all done, I could finally get creative and start thinking about how to decorate the space.

Decor

This was the first room where I used wallpaper across the whole room. I'd not tried it properly before, other than in smaller areas like the ceiling to the party room or in the little toilet space in the pink bathroom (and, indeed, in my first house, I'd never used any pattern at all, other than rugs and the odd cushion), so this felt like a big step and was a bit daunting – especially in such a large room – but the space was crying out for it and, emboldened by my work with Anna Hayman (see page 145), I went for it. I absolutely fell in love with a particular design that has its origins in the Coromandel coastline in India (India is one of my favourite places in the world and I think that's why I love a lot of the pattern and print that comes from there) where exotic chintz were printed from the mid-seventeenth century for a European audience.

There's a funny (and slightly embarrassing) story about the paper ... I'd actually been working with Warner House right at the start of them coming back to the market (it's an incredible brand with amazing history that can be traced all the way back to the sixteenth century – they've woven articles for every coronation since 1902 and were even involved in the 1902 refurbishment of the White House) – and they'd sent me pre-production wallpaper. All their rolls now come with information with instructions on which way to hang it, but mine didn't and, upon looking at the pattern, I installed it the way that made sense to me. Well, it turns out I'm a bit of a daft apeth and got it wrong, merrily hanging it upside down around the whole room – what a wally! In my defence, it's a mythical tree, not designed to be true to life, and there are elements in it that definitely look right this way up (to me at least). Regardless of its orientation, I love it and think it looks grand this way round. I did panic marginally when I realised that

Warner House were going to want to use images of the space to help promote their glorious wares, and upside down wallpaper probably isn't ideal, and that I might, therefore, have to strip it all off and start again. Thankfully, they were so very wonderful about it and we all had a jolly good chuckle – they even tried to take some of the blame with it being a pre-production run ... all's well that ends well.

I believe the bay window in this room, mirroring the two circular bays on the floors below, is a later addition. I have no paperwork or similar to prove this, but it's the only part of the building that isn't made from stone. My hunch is that this room would have once stopped at the panelled archway, with a large window there possibly then stepping out on to the flat roof of the bay, but for some reason this was added.

Unlike pretty much every other external wall in the house which is made of stone and then has a very large, well-ventilated cavity before the lath and plaster finish to stop any moisture from the external walls coming through into the interior (unless sopping wet from a leak or damage!), this room has plaster applied straight to the wall and had, over the years, been concreted and plastered over, stopping it from breathing. The wall was very wet (again, that pesky blocked gutter) so there was a lot to put right, taking away inappropriate material and replacing it with something breathable.

I was worried that wallpaper would impair the new breathability of the bay window and ultimately peel itself off, so I painted the bay the same colour as the woodwork in here – a sort of fawny brown ('Mudlark' by Fenwick & Tilbrook) – but then used the same print as the wallpaper in a fabric in the form of a wide Roman blind that links the two spaces really nicely.

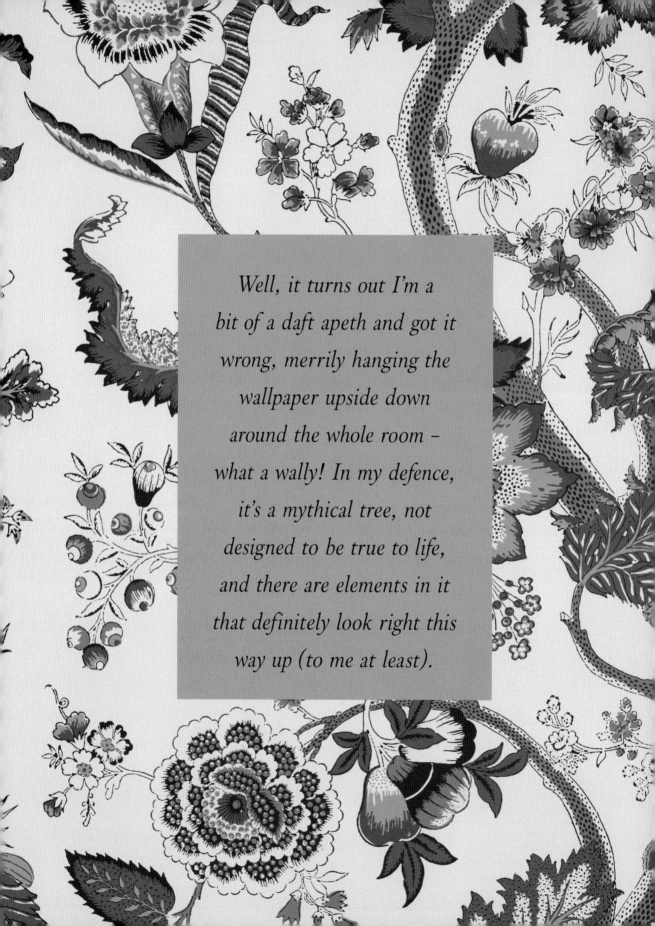

Well, it turns out I'm a bit of a daft apeth and got it wrong, merrily hanging the wallpaper upside down around the whole room – what a wally! In my defence, it's a mythical tree, not designed to be true to life, and there are elements in it that definitely look right this way up (to me at least).

The room did (and still does) have a fireplace. Sadly, at some point the original Georgian fireplace, which would have been fairly large in a room this size, was ripped out and replaced with a tiny, 1930s cast-iron combination fireplace. It's a pretty thing, but totally inappropriate in size and design for the room and looks a bit silly. I therefore decided to restore the fireplace, but then cover it up, using that space positioned between two very old cupboards built into the alcoves, to place a large, statement headboard, inspired by the bedrooms in the

hotels Kit Kemp designs and creates. I wanted a real focal point for the room and, with such a large pattern on the walls, I went with a dark, rich, forest-green velvet adorned with large brass studs.

Now, an 8-foot (2.4-metre) headboard isn't the sort of thing you can just wander down into town and pick up. At this point, I'd never even thought about upholstery, let alone tried my hand at it. But, with again an entirely misplaced sense of self-confidence, I assumed it would be straightforward and cracked on.

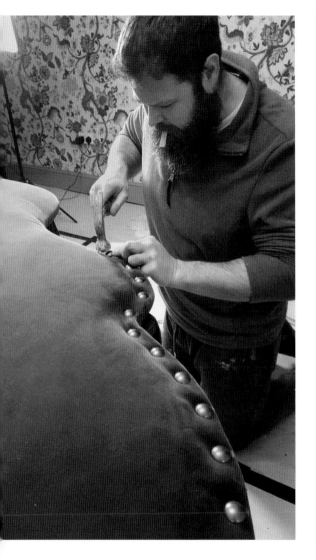

It turns out, in this instance, unlike pretty much everything else I seem to have a go at, apart from some head scratching around the internal corners and the fact that it definitely doesn't look pretty from the back (but that's just between you and me ... OK?), it was actually quite straightforward. Plywood, a staple gun, the fabric, foam, a hammer – and you're pretty much away. Overall, for not a lot of brass, I ended up with something bespoke for the space that looks and feels very high-end and definitely does as I'd hoped it would. (And I'm pleased to report that, three years on, the headboard still looks as good as new!)

I added a simple, sprung divan base, and, with my chief sewer (my ma) too far away to be of use at this point, a wonderful local seamstress created a matching valance from the same material for the bed, which makes it all feel very opulent and luxurious.

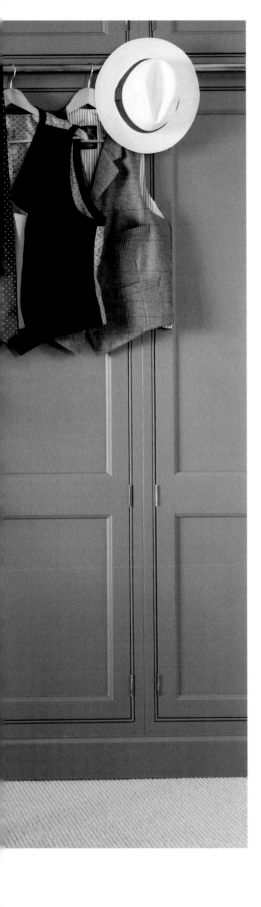

Furniture

The final big piece in the space was the wardrobes. This is one of the few bedrooms that actually has a flat wall that can take a decent-sized wardrobe (that isn't the only place in the room I can put a bed), so I decided that, as well as a very infrequently-used guest bedroom (this one being darker and at the back of the house), I'd also turn this room into my dressing room of sorts (as there is no place to store my clothes in my bedroom, as I've mentioned previously).

On the top floor, in the eaves that would have been the servants' living quarters I believe, is a beautiful, old, built-in housekeeper's cupboard. I wanted to create something similar to this, but a little more refined to suit this grander, more ornate space. I came up with some rough ideas and Howard at Heaven and Stubbs (the same guys that made the kitchen – see page 77) came up with something really beautiful. Made from solid beech, with bespoke pale oak internals, and painted a warm, earthy pinky-red – 'Highland Peat' from Fenwick & Tilbrook – they're a thing of beauty and wouldn't look out of place on Saville Row; if only I could say the same about my clothes!

We decided to add a brass rail across the front. Initially this was purely a spot to rest the oak ladders Howard made, to ease access to the top cupboards, but, in practice, it's become a wonderful spot to hang outfits, air clothes and is so useful – I can't believe it's not standard fit on all wardrobes (how often do you put a hanger over the back of a door or similar?). Wonderfully, it's a feature that Howard has been asked to install on a number of cupboards since.

Finishing Touches

The lighting starts with a statement, antique, mirrored pendant. The ceilings, while not low, aren't the highest, especially given the size of the room. So I needed something big enough to have some impact and not looked lost against the ceiling, but without too low a drop, and this piece from Pooky feels perfect in the space. Sweet little marbled wall lights either side of the bed make the space feel cosy at night, with lamps dotted around to create gentle pools of light. The thickest, squidgiest wool carpet beneath your feet does the same and makes the room wonderfully hushed.

I've yet to properly do much with the bay window end. I think I need some more storage and furniture in there, but I've added a sofa as, when you're this high up, the view out the back is really lovely indeed.

Despite all this hard work, the name has stuck. It always catches people by surprise – they look at me a bit funny when they walk into the room for the first time and I introduce it nonchalantly as 'The Room of Doom'; I usually have to show photos of what it first looked like. When it comes to the smell of pigeons, thankfully they need to use their imagination for that (or head to the floor above!).

THE SLOW EVOLUTION OF
THE ROOM – WITH LIGHT
REFRESHMENTS

It's a very nice spot to relax and watch the birds come and go on an evening as the sun goes down.

WALLPAPER

Wallpaper seems to accentuate the nice architectural features too, like fireplaces, windows and cornicing, while disguising any lumps and bumps on the walls.

I'm sure you've noticed by now that there's a bit of a running theme throughout lots of the completed rooms, in that an awful lot of them have wallpaper, and I thought my thoughts on wallpaper deserve their own section.

I should probably confess to having been a complete novice when buying Admirals. Not only had I never used wallpaper before, but my last home didn't really have any pattern of which to speak. Pattern actually made me nervous and I assumed that it would be horribly complicated to make it work in a space: that wallpaper would be hard to install, that it would make the room feel small, busy and annoying and that I might tire of it quickly – I'd convinced myself it wasn't for me. However, as I started researching interiors of Georgian houses and the interior designers whose rooms I admired, wallpaper was a bit of a running theme and so I decided to give it a whirl.

I came to realise that wallpapering a room is probably the single biggest thing you can do to really elevate it. It's also remarkable what wallpaper physically does to spaces – rather than making them feel small and busy, as I'd feared, it seems to make them feel larger and taller, giving the walls depth, drawing the eye around the room and up to the ceiling. Alas, Admirals didn't come with any old masters hanging on the wall either, so, while I've a modest and slowly growing collection of slightly ramshackle artwork, wallpaper really helps if you've not got a pile of beautifully framed pieces to adorn plainer walls.

Wallpaper seems to accentuate the nice architectural features too, like fireplaces, windows and cornicing, while disguising any lumps and bumps on the walls, or even awkward angles and boxes you might have for pipes and vents. It can bring a softness to a room, almost a warmth, and seems to help the acoustics ever so slightly (though this could just be in my head). It also feels warmer to the touch than bare, painted walls (though, if you're visiting, please keep one's greasy paws off my wallpaper – ha ha!).

Wallpapering is also far easier than I thought it would be. Using good-quality paper and making sure that you paste the wall rather than soaking the paper makes things far easier. (Pa gave me a hand for a couple of hours once. Having previously found wallpapering to be a pain worse than death that may or may not have nearly led to divorce, he couldn't believe how simple I was making it look – he surmised that the quality of the paper made the difference, saying his had ripped like tissue paper the second he tried to manipulate it – though he's blessed with a similar ham-fisted nature to me!) The main thing is to use a snap blade knife, and snap before pretty much every cut to give crisp cuts without any pulls or tears. Take your time, watch lots of YouTube videos beforehand and you'll be fine. (A laser level and a tripod also make life far, far easier.)

It's also worth pointing out that wallpaper is

far more forgiving than people might think. If your pattern doesn't expertly match going round a corner, or you find it's not perfectly level (both of which are applicable in literally every single room I've wallpapered), no one will ever know – in fact, after a little while, you'll struggle to spot the flaws yourself.

As for patterns and what to choose, going with something that is reasonably period-appropriate will probably give you a very good chance of it feeling 'right' in the space. It almost makes it (nearly) impossible for it to date given it's already old and has probably come in and out of fashion ten times ... but the most important thing is for you to love it.

When using wallpaper, I would strongly recommend taking the pattern right around the room. An exception to this would be something like a large, bespoke mural – not something I've (as yet at least) used, but I would treat that more like a wall-sized piece of art rather than wallpaper specifically. In my mind, a 'feature' wall, whether in paint or paper, makes the room look bitty, busy and cluttered and doesn't feel at all harmonious.

BEDROOM
Four

Firstly, apologies if the numbering for these rooms doesn't seem to make a lot of sense ... it's simply the numbers on the brass plaques above the doors put there by the navy. My bedroom on the first floor is '1' and the pink bathroom adjacent to it is '2'. The 'Room of Doom' is actually '3', but I tried calling it that and it didn't stick!

A Suite *fit for*...
an Admiral

OR JUST MY PALS!

All of the bedrooms on the top two floors have a similar plaque. I'm not entirely sure whether this was to remind the household staff which room was which or to help guests find their room when staying, given the slightly transient nature of military houses with lots of occupants, but it's a sweet little feature that I'll be restoring – if I ever make it on to the hallways and landings, that is.

This would be what I would class as the principal guest bedroom. Being the largest of the guest spaces at the front of the house, it gets the most light and has the best fireplace too (more on that to follow). It's also attached, again in a Jack and Jill configuration, to another room, the original purpose of which I'm not sure of. It was possibly a nursery attached to the main bedroom or maybe a dressing room. Either way, I've turned it into a semi-bathroom-cum-dressing room, with a basin and free-standing bath, so it made sense to make this the main guest room – there's rather a luxurious feel to it when taken as a suite.

As in so many of the front rooms of the house, there are three beautiful sash windows, albeit this time smaller in proportion to reflect the lower ceilings and without the panelling and shutters found in the lower levels of the house. Being further up seems to affect the quality of the light – the angle at which the sun comes in and the lack of shadows as it dips behind buildings that cast their outlines further down the house give these rooms an almost ethereal quality.

Headboards can help to create impact and make
the bed the centre of attention in a bedroom.

Decor

The room feels a bit unfinished at the minute, as do a lot, as I tend to get the renovating and decorating done and then the finishing touches can come in time as I plough on with the graft in the next room. It's a little bare as it stands and needs more furniture and what not, but the starting point, as is often the way, was the beautiful wallpaper.

It's an interpretation of an eighteenth-century Chinese paper, and looks almost mythical, with beautiful colours against a neutral backdrop, once again from Warner House. I paired it with a soft, muted putty on the woodwork called 'Little Donkey' from Fenwick & Tilbrook (it just seems to work really well in houses of this age) and an embroidered fabric on both the curtains and another enormous headboard I upholstered to really ground the bed in such a big space.

But the thing I love the most in this room are a pair of cabinets I bought from auction that I think would have once graced a grand dining room. They are so beautifully made and really feel like 'antiques of the future', being, I believe, only maybe fifty years old. The almost jade green marble slabs on the top pair beautifully with the wallpaper and fabric and tie in with the Asian feel.

Add a brass chandelier with shades and another super squidgy woollen carpet that adds quiet luxury, and the whole space has a light, calming feel.

The fireplace was the starting point for the whole space once I'd uncovered the beautiful marble. With few other features, it really makes a statement and it informed my choices everywhere else in the space.

The Fireplace

The fireplace in this room was very unloved when I got to it. The later (1910ish I think) cast-iron insert was rusty and incomplete, and the tiles were cracked and broken, with some missing. The surround, yet again, had been painted over and over again, eventually with a white matt emulsion for some reason. I had scraped a bit off when first moving in so I knew it was some kind of dark stone, but the bit I'd scraped back was a dull, flat grey with no markings. I assumed it was slate, and would have been

more than happy with it as such. However, when I added the Kling Strip to it (see page 116 for the wonders of this stuff) and waited the agonising 48 hours for it to work its magic, what I found was … beautiful, veined marble. I believe it is 'Ashburton' marble, which would make sense as it's a local marble. Black, with veins of white and red, it gave a slightly Chinese feel which went beautifully with the paper. It was a huge amount of work to restore (especially as it'll certainly never be lit), but is such a

beautiful focal point given the room is void of much else in the way of original features.

I added tiles appropriate to the period of the insert, if not the house, made locally in Exeter by Original Style, which actually started life as a tile maker, specifically making tiles for cast-iron fireplace maker Stovax, also based in Devon. I also added hearth tiles – again, while it wasn't going to be a functional fireplace, I at least wanted it to look functional, as I always want fireplaces to (I find

it really odd when people take carpet or wood floors into and over where the hearth should be) – and it set the fireplace off beautifully.

This room was used as my bedroom when I first moved in, being the cleanest in the house (a very relative term!) and it really is a lovely space, with light pouring in on a morning with views over the square and beyond. Family and friends always seem to sleep well in here too, which I'll take as a good sign.

The Yellow Bathroom

The half-bathroom of sorts next door, with its Jack and Jill doors, did have a basin in the corner, but that doesn't tell you all that much as all the rooms on this floor had basins in them. It did mean, however, that there was a lead waste pipe exiting out of the front of the house for grey water – though obviously not a full soil pipe, so it was never going to be possible to add a lavatory in here. Putting in a bath, with the help of a water lifting station and utilising the old waste pipe, at least gave the room some purpose, while still leaving plenty of space for an old wardrobe to create a sort of dressing room for guests and giving them somewhere to get washed up and brush their teeth without needing to use the main bathroom if there are a few people staying.

I panelled the lower portion of the walls with a wide Georgian-style bead and butt panelling. It's made from moisture-resistant MDF from The English Panelling Company and, once primed and painted, is perfect for bathrooms. I restored the floors, first sanding them smooth and filling any holes and sealing the cracks, and then painting them with a chequerboard design which was a bit of a head scratcher, but still looks great a couple of years on. To get the squares perfect, you have to use painters' masking tape. A good trick to get a clean edge when using tape is to paint the whole floor first in the base colour. In this instance, I painted the whole floor pale, and then 'drew' on the squares with the tape. I then painted the edges of the tape where the blue would be with the pale colour and let it dry. This effectively seals any areas of the tape that might not be quite sealed tight, where you'd otherwise see the blue bleeding through. Once it was dry, I painted on the blue, and the edges are absolutely perfect. I always remove the tape when the last coat of paint is still wet and it seems to work a treat.

The bath, which I restored and painted, was second-hand from eBay and, for the basin, I chose a wonderfully whimsical bowl, complete with fish that, when it's full, look like they're swimming in the water. I sat it on an old pine drawer that I converted to take the waste pipes, cutting out part of the internal drawer so it would still function, while allowing the basin's trap through. I also boxed around the pipework so I could wall-mount the taps.

The chandelier I installed was another I restored from one of the other rooms in the house with a rewire and the crystals cleaned up (and far enough from the sources of water that it didn't need to be a specific bathroom fitting), which always helps a room to feel a bit less sterile and adds a little vintage sparkle and glamour. I also installed a brass ship light either side of the mirror.

The old Victorian wardrobe (which might actually be a compactum, though I'm not sure on the exact definition) that has the original mercury mirror in the door adds a bit of antique texture, and, overall, the room flows really nicely from the bedroom it's attached to while still feeling like its own space.

INSPIRATION

I'm asked quite a bit where I find my inspiration. I'd love to be able to tell you a romantic tale of how it's the colours of nature, or the crashing waves of the sea, or some other similarly lovely notion. Alas, while I know that works for some, mine is a little more like graft, but it seems to work for me. I know there are some who also say that beautiful hotels and similar provide inspiration, but, while I'm sure they can, nights I've spent in very fancy hotels can be counted on one hand, and in a tent on a campsite in the hundreds, so it very much depends on your lifestyle and budget.

I've already taken you through a little of how I actually pull together a space, but before all that comes the research – hours and hours of it. I would never call myself an interior designer – my process for finding ideas and inspiration for a space is much simpler and more pragmatic, and I certainly don't feel like I'm trying to create something no one has ever seen before; I'm just trying to turn a lovely, if a bit knackered, pile of stone into my home. To do this, I look at lots and lots (and lots) of images and pictures, hunting down elements of spaces and rooms I like, and squirreling them away until I've got enough to create a cohesive space.

Obviously with the interweb this is pretty straightforward, though usually my starting point is interiors magazines – think of these as curated collections that might help you find your style in the first instance. For me, it's the likes of *House & Gardens* and *The English Home* as these will then potentially expose you to some designers whose taste and work you enjoy. Now, thanks to Instagram and Google, you essentially have an enormous collection of their back catalogue at your fingertips to delve into. Instagram is a great place for this, as, once you start, it'll serve you more and more similar inspiration to farm.

There are, of course, some rules when it comes to styling, and definitely some of them are worth breaking too, but you could do far worse than run through what Kate Watson-Smyth (@mad_about_the_house) has to say about most subjects. You don't have to like her taste necessarily, but the basic principles of design, which I think she's brilliant at getting across, apply no matter what your style; the size of rugs, proportion and scale … that sort of thing.

BEDROOM
Seven

This room is a little smaller than the others, with only two windows across rather than three and is roughly 16 by 16 feet (4.9 by 4.9 metres). There was a boarded-up fireplace and a built-in cupboard when I moved in, but not much more as a starting point for this space. It's a lovely light, bright room, though, with a really nice feel and is often guests' favourite room. I think after some of the grander, bigger spaces, to come in here (now it's finished at least!), it feels quite cosy and modest and homely. I do, however, know that at some time around 1900, it was used as a child's room or nursery, as under the floor I found offcuts of a children's wallpaper from that era that matched some kept in the Victoria and Albert museum archives, showing various figurines with letters of the alphabet.

First Things
First

The first job in this room was to see what was hiding behind the board covering the fireplace ... well, there was a LOT of dust and dirt, along with the skeletons of many, many birds, but I was thrilled to see the original cast-iron insert hadn't been removed, though it had, of course, been painted over and over again with gloss paint. (My first home had all the fireplaces ripped out before my ownership, and I spent hours and hours searching for salvaged replacements to give the rooms their heart back, so it was heartening that I didn't need to do the same here). Sadly, the simple wooden fireplace surround had been damaged over the years so needed replacing, and there was an awkward-looking section at the top which meant the insert didn't fully fill the surround.

I got going with stripping the insert and getting it all polished up and restored, replaced the hearth with a simple piece of marble and added beautiful hand-painted delft-style tiles, with a fitting nautical theme, to cover the space at the top – and the room had its focal point back.

There was a very old, inbuilt cupboard in the corner that needed a bit of work to get it functioning right and the usual radiators to replace, but, all in all, it wasn't the most difficult room in the house to get prepped.

Furnishings

As in many of the other rooms, the first thing I decided on was the wallpaper, and I wanted something a little softer and more gentle than the bolder, bigger prints used elsewhere, which felt right with it being a slightly smaller space.

This is a scrolling, linear fern design with the print having been taken from an eighteenth-century girl's dress – so again in terms of the pattern it's quite period-appropriate to the house. The wallpaper adds depth and interest, and adds to that warm, cosy feeling.

A few pieces of vintage furniture and an old brass bed (sadly now gone – it was bought second-hand and, alas, it gave way) gave the room a very timeless feel. My folks were using this room to store one of their beds over the summer and I used it for some of these photos, hence there being a couple of different beds in the shots, but I think I'll try to replace the brass bed or maybe upholster another headboard. They work so well in the other rooms and have almost become a bit of a signature look to the bedrooms here.

I went with neutral linen curtains to give the eye a bit of a calm space to rest, though they're embellished with beautiful onions down the side to add a bit of interest and tie in the blue colour, and the pinch pleat is an elegant detail.

Cosy carpet, layered with a rug and a simple glass pendant, combined with lots of lamps, finish off the space nicely and it does have a really welcoming feel.

The wallpaper is a scrolling, linear fern design with the print having been taken from an eighteenth-century girl's dress.

The CHINESE BATHROOM

THE

SECOND

FLOOR

The floorplan of this space is identical to that of the pink bathroom below it, including the quirky curved space for the lavatory, albeit with lower ceilings and fewer grand features, as with the other rooms on this floor. There's a door from Bedroom Seven leading into it and it also has the twin of the fireplace in that little room (in equally grim condition). When I first moved in, this room was in a bit of a sorry state, full of rot, strange 1960s built-in furniture and pipes everywhere.

It's All *in* *the* Detail

WITH LOTS TO REPAIR

This room had obviously been used as a bathroom for many decades. There was a cast-iron bath in here that I believe would have been from around the 1920s based on its style, though it was absolutely knackered and so small I couldn't get my shoulders in it without hunching over, being almost coffin-shaped. Then, in the 1960s (and I could date it to that as I found newspaper with the date on used as filler and packing as I started taking it apart), someone decided to try to modernise it by boxing it in, and then adding a shower. Well, it would be fair to say that boxing in a cast-iron roll top bath, and putting a shower above it, using plywood probably isn't the best idea and, inevitably, water had been cascading into places it very much shouldn't for decades. As a result, the carpet had sort of fused to the floorboards. The curtain rail, though, was a bit of a stroke of genius – obviously being the site of a hospital, the beds would have had curtains around them, and some clever soul went and borrowed one from the hospital to use for the Admirals shower; brilliant, though, alas, a feature I wasn't all that keen on keeping!

There was a lot to unpick in this space before I started bringing it back together. On deciding to lay solid oak parquet, the first job was to level the floor. Given the state of the floorboards, most of these weren't salvageable anyway, so I took them all up and then added sister joists to the current joists. The sister joists allowed me to level out the very significant unevenness of the floor, ahead of then adding the parquet over the top. The parquet is again made by Broadleaf Timber in Wales, and this is their aged oak. Each solid oak piece is aged by hand to give the immediate appearance that it's been laid a long time and it works beautifully. With this bathroom again facing north, I wanted to use the oak to add some warmth to the space, both visually with the beautiful honey tones of the oak, and practically, oak being far cosier on your toes than tiles. A lot of people were surprised with me using oak in a bathroom, but it's worth remembering that wood, especially oak, which is incredibly dense, is absolutely fine with water – so long as you're a) sensible (and aren't trying to use it in a wet room), and b) look after it – we make boats out of it after all!

Levelling the floor and adding the sister joists was an absolute monster of a job working alone – really properly grim and not something I'd look forward to doing again if I had to – but, once the floor was level and boarded using NoMorePly (a tile backing board system that is a lot thinner than plywood or chipboard for the same strength) to lessen the height once the parquet was added, actually laying the parquet itself was a breeze and definitely something DIYable.

After that, I attached panelling on the lower half of the walls and higher behind the bath to act as a splashback and help frame the bath between the two doors, with a peg rail above giving handy hanging options for wet towels, and so on. I painted the panelling in a washable eggshell finish with a whimsical late eighteenth-century chinoiserie-style fishing scene above to add a little fun and interest in the plainer space.

I used a punchy cerise eggshell paint on the bath that really pops and is picked up by some wall lamp shades. I've also added an old chair, rug and towel rail to add further texture, as well as art and ceramics.

I used handmade, patterned tiles for the shower (with a visually light enclosure that blends into the background as best it can). I had hoped that, by using patterned tiles in a similar colour to the wallpaper, the eye would again read it all as one, cohesive space without drawing too much attention to itself, while still being beautiful in itself, and I feel this has worked really well.

Another high-level cistern for the WC completes the room, and makes a statement of its own, working beautifully in the space.

Again, the end result is one of quiet, relaxed comfort, not immediately apparent as a bathroom but simply a warm, interesting, comfortable space for whiling away an hour or two with a hot bath (or, you know, brushing your teeth!).

The
THIRD
FLOOR

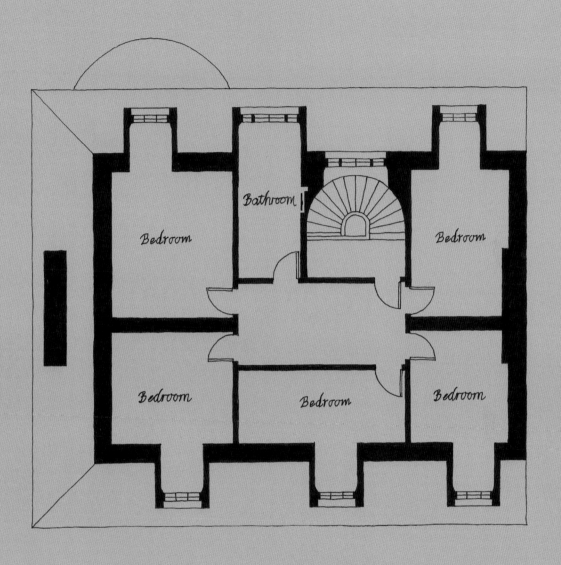

Bathroom

Bedroom

Bedroom

Bedroom

Bedroom

Bedroom

Third Floor Plan

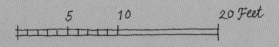

5   10   20 Feet

A Long Way Up

WITH VIEWS TO MATCH

Currently, all I've done up here is fix leaks and rip out a very badly fitted bathroom (partly responsible for some of the leaks further down the house), but it's a really interesting floor. Once, it would have been the bedrooms of the household staff and I'm told they would have likely considered themselves fairly lucky, as these rooms have fireplaces meaning they could be heated – not always a given with servants' quarters (though perhaps not so lucky given it would have been their own legs running the coal up and down the seventy or so stairs between this floor and the coal vaults beneath the road).

When I looked round there were four people sharing this floor, with another on the floor below. With it being rented out on a very ad-hoc, by-room basis, there was also a makeshift kitchen and living room in one of the rooms and the aforementioned leaking bathroom between them.

This space is very restricted in terms of its head height (I have to duck to get through the doorways) and built into the eaves of the house, with extraordinary, curved dormer windows in five of the rooms. The windows themselves pivot on a central hinge and aren't in great shape – they're going to need a lot of attention one day and the wind currently howls through them! Various homemade draught-proofing measures remain in evidence around the windows and doors.

I'm not fully sure how I'll use these spaces yet. I've no desperate need for further bedrooms in the main house, though one or two will likely become bedrooms. Indeed, there are some people, when they come to look round the house, who prefer the feel on this floor to any other, being much simpler and cosier, so it'd be nice to have that to offer friends when they come to stay.

Another one or two rooms will become, I think, dressing rooms of sorts – glorified storage really given there's limited storage elsewhere in the rooms (and not much of a loft to speak of) – but made pretty ... a useful space to keep things organised and in place. I'll also reinstate the bathroom, which has a much larger dormer window with fantastic views which, being so far up, stretch out over Plymouth and across to what would have been the old military hospital (once home to the longest colonnade in Europe). I'd also like a space for a music room to keep a drum kit and some general paraphernalia not really bonny enough to be on display in the rest of the house. Overall, though, it's one of the last spaces I'll finish in the whole house, though it'll need doing before I tackle the hall, stairs and landing spaces (which I'll come on to on page 230).

THE WHOLE HOUSE HAS
NEEDED REWIRING

The
LOWER
GROUND
FLOOR

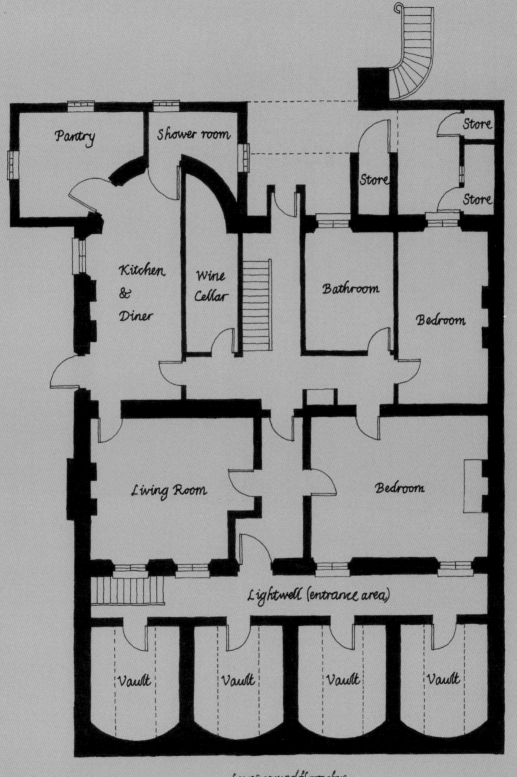

Pantry

Shower room

Store

Store

Store

Kitchen & Diner

Wine Cellar

Bathroom

Bedroom

Living Room

Bedroom

Lightwell (entrance area)

Vault

Vault

Vault

Vault

Lower ground floor plan

5   10   20 Feet

The SERVANTS' QUARTERS

THE LOWER GROUND FLOOR

We've been through what would have been the 'main' house, starting on the ground floor and working our way up. We're now diving down into the hard-working belly of the house ...

Potential

AND LOTS OF WORK!

The lower ground, a space where the staff would have worked, cooked and generally run the house from, as well as likely lived in part, is an almost entirely separate space from the rest of the house. With its own entrance, it is accessed from the front via some granite steps leading to the space in front of the coal vaults beneath the road and a walkway between them and the house. These spaces were some of the most derelict when I first got the keys and in a really shocking state, especially at the back of the house. Bits of work had been done, incredibly badly, to some of it (all of which needs removing and making good as it's a real mess and potentially causing further damage to the house), but others were a wet, rotten, rubble-strewn disaster.

Taken as a whole, there's quite a lot of space down here, occupying a similar square footage to most four-bedroomed houses. Obviously, with a distinct lack of any household staff around these parts (alas), it seems ridiculous having it sitting there unused, so my intention in the longer run is to create a sympathetic, luxurious holiday let for people to come and enjoy a little slice of Admirals House and the delights of Devon and Cornwall. The old hospital site is a beautiful, quiet place to spend a few days while being a stone's throw from both the sea and the centre of Plymouth itself.

This will also help to maintain and run the house, and gives me good reason to keep it warm and loved down here, which is always good for a house, making sure it stays in good order and any damp kept at bay.

There is sadly a distinct lack of anything that tells me much about its past down here in terms of its time spent working hard to keep the Admiral and his family fed, clothed and warm. I am hoping I might find a little more as I unpick some of the changes, but it looks as though most bits were ripped out a long time ago. Albert and his daughters told me that, in their time here, this area was used primarily for storage, and also as a sort of makeshift workshop (the kitchen had already been moved to the ground floor for Albert to use – see page 24) – they didn't remember seeing any old fireplaces or ranges or worktables or similar. The old floors, a mixture

of stone flags and wood I believe (more investigation is required), have largely had concrete poured over them and what looks a bit like a sort of bitumen which I'm sure is going to be lots of fun to remove. Where services for the 'main house' were required, little thought was given to the routes of pipes or cables, with ceiling heights restricted in places and holes bashed through walls with merry abandon.

All in all, it's a bit of a state. It's the space I'll be working on next though. I have already restored two rooms and the back hall connecting them, so have made a bit of a head start.

They were utility and laundry spaces when I looked around, if you can call them such – again, a variety of creatures were found as I was clearing up and they were so chock-full of 'stuff' that you couldn't really get in them. Indeed, in the centre of the room that's now a little bedroom, there was an absolutely huge, ancient cast-iron boiler that was so surrounded by detritus on viewing, I

had no idea it was even there! My pa came to have a look to help work out how on earth we might be able to remove it, knowing it was well beyond me to lift on my own. Of course, not only would it have been far too big to fit through the door or window, but it must have weighed well over a ton and had been cemented into place.

Being the age it was, and decades since it was likely last fired up (thankfully all the pipes had been disconnected, including the massive, asbestos flue), all the cast-iron components, likely built one piece at a time in place, were seized together. In the end, we decided the only thing to do was to get some goggles on and hit it with a massive hammer, finally earning my Instagram handle! Cast iron is remarkably brittle, almost smashing like very thick, heavy glass. It was a very messy job, but in not too long a time we were able to load up a wheelbarrow and cart it out.

These spaces (given the proximity to the old and more recent boilers) were the worst affected in terms of the pipes and services running across the ceilings. While theoretically it would have been possible to reroute them, through ceiling voids and so on, it would have been very expensive, time-consuming and also quite damaging to the original fabric of the house. I decided simply to baton it out and install a false ceiling, hiding the pipework and adding an additional layer of sound and fire insulation, which was relatively straightforward to achieve. It does mean that things are quite snug in these spaces in terms of head height, but it sort of adds to that servants' quarters feel.

In the new spaces I've done down here – namely the back hallway and the bathroom – you'll see that, despite my mention of them not being my favourite things in the world, I've used spotlights. In spaces with such restrictive head height there's a limit to what else you can do, though; had I been doing the work now, I'd have

introduced wall lighting into the hallway, albeit at extra cost. The other rooms in the lower ground had already been semi-converted, complete with spotlight grids in the ceiling. As I get round to renovating these areas, I'll likely keep some of the spotlights, but move them closer to the walls, as the ceiling height is low in here too – but there certainly don't need to be quite so many. Spotlights, when used thoughtfully, can be great problem-solvers.

I've deliberately not 'over-restored' these spaces. There's a big, smooth, worn area on the bottom of the door from the back hall into the now bathroom. Clearly caused by probably 150 years of someone going in and out with armfuls of stuff, using their feet to open and close it, it's absolutely charming and the sort of thing I want to retain in these spaces.

I BUILT THE BATH AROUND THE
REMAINS OF THE WALL SO AS
NOT TO DISTURB THE ORIGINAL
FABRIC OF THE BUILDING

The Bathroom

The bathroom already had plumbing and drainage, but it still caused some interesting challenges, not least of all the rubbly remains of an old wall that would, I believe, have once been a support for the original staircase. It is, in part, still in use, with joists above resting on it, so I simply cleared up the loose bits and decided the only course of action was to work around it.

I managed to work out, once I'd tiled, that if I bought the shortest bath I could sensibly find, I could just squeeze it in, with a shower over the top. Then, using the back, angled wall facing the window, I added the basin here. It sounds weird, but actually works really well – with an enclosed bath/shower and the mirror above the basin reflecting the light from the window – and it's all certainly a bit quirky.

There was an old wall cupboard I restored and an old towel rail on the back of the door that came in very handy. All the fixtures and fittings from this little room were bought off Facebook Marketplace for peanuts and I think the cost of doing this whole space (excluding my labour of course) was around £500.

It's not the most glamorous bathroom in the world, and the pictures here are looking quite plain – when I did it, it was primarily so a friend had somewhere to stay, and I didn't at that time know the longer-term goal for the lower ground, thinking likely I'd use it as a longer-term let, but given I'm now one day hoping to use it as a holiday let, I think I'd like to make it a little more in keeping with the rest of Admirals (though, alas, I can't make it any bigger!) so it'll need art and dressing and likely a little more decoration to make it more special before it's ready for guests. However, it has a lovely feel to it and it's appropriate for the floor it's on.

The Bedroom

Initially, I restored this to a functional state, using the same colours and basic style as the back hall and bathroom, but once it was no longer needed by my friend, I had the opportunity to add a few smarter finishing touches. It's obviously not huge (and was once home to the aforementioned old boiler), but might, of all the rooms, have had the biggest makeover in terms of before and afters. It doesn't get a lot of light, being right in the belly of the house at the back, looking out on to an old courtyard, but that does mean it's incredibly quiet and peaceful and a great spot for a lie-in.

I used a simple repeating patterned wallpaper to inject some character (and it made the room feel a little bigger). It also disguised some of the odd shapes in here too. I've added some colourful furniture and art and, well, it's a really sweet little room. As with everywhere, it needs a few finishing touches, but it's the perfect spot for a few nights – though I'm not sure whether, when I rent out the apartment, it's likely to be to people who require two bedrooms – we shall see!

Through my Instagram account, it's wonderful how many people seem nearly as enchanted as I am with this place and it'll be lovely to be able to share it with them in some way.

The Wine Cellar

Alongside the bathroom and little bedroom, the back hall leads to the very much unrestored wine cellar ... and there's certainly no wine in it (chance would be a fine thing!). It's 24 feet (7.3 metres) long, with the classic brick and slate bins for the wine. Of course, it's all been painted in many, many layers of magnolia paint and clearly has been this way for many years as I've a photograph back when Albert was quite a young man, decanting some kind of spirit from a demijohn with everything in the same colour.

There's pipework everywhere and, interestingly, the remains of a window on the rear, curved wall. It's this that makes me think the spaces beyond it, that make up the rooms below the roof terrace that the set of double doors in the kitchen on the ground floor lead out on to, aren't original and are likely a Victorian addition. Again, there's a huge amount to do in here, but while it's definitely not high on my list of priorities, I will absolutely make it beautiful again – one day!

The Main Bedroom

At the front of the lower ground, there's a very large room that will become a bedroom. Again, there seems to be evidence of a separate door leading outside, so this room would have had its own entrance and exit, making me wonder whether this was perhaps the living quarters of a butler or the head of the household staff in some way. It has quite a grand fireplace, and would have been very comfortable. It's directly in the centre of the house too so would have been a good place to keep an eye on the comings and goings of things. Ceiling heights in the spaces from here on in are better as there's far less in the way of services running across it all. Also, being at the front of the house, despite being 'below ground',

the south-facing sash windows mean the rooms don't feel too dark or gloomy.

There are lots of built-in cupboards and storage that will be restored, alongside the fireplace, and it should make quite a grand, luxurious bedroom when it's finished. Being the principal bedroom down here, I definitely want to introduce a healthy dose of pattern and colour as I have upstairs to give people the full Admirals experience, and it's easiest to do that in a bedroom than any other really, especially one of this size, as it doesn't need to be a terribly functional room, and there are lots of reasons to layer up fabrics and prints.

The Living Room

From here, the front hall leads to what will be the living room. Again, two south-facing sash windows mean it's surprisingly light and bright, but gosh this room has been botched plenty. There's some slightly odd, bulky modern built-in shelving that I can only assume was built to hide something behind that was beyond restoring – I cannot wait to rip them out and see what I'm working with. The laminate flooring moves and twists as you walk on it because whatever is underneath isn't solid. The fireplace is truly awful and needs putting back to something far more in keeping with the space – it will all be removed back to the original material, if indeed I can find it.

Again, though, it's a good space and one that will be very comfortable for guests when they come and stay by the time I'm finished with it. There is, of course, the obligatory paint-stripping needed, windows to repair and panelling and architrave to put right, but there are some quite nice little details once they're restored that will make it quite special.

I rather like the idea of trying to find an old range to fit the space – it wouldn't be functional, but would look the part.

The Kitchen

The living room leads through into the kitchen. A really nice space, this room sits below the ground floor kitchen in the same configuration, but cut down the middle at the two-thirds mark (the other side of that wall is the wine cellar). On the surface, this doesn't look too bad. It's got everything a kitchen needs, but again, when you look closely, it's been so badly done. There's lots to the fabric of the space that needs sorting properly. For instance, the door to the garden is rotten, badly fitted and lets in a gale. The room doesn't have any heating other than the Aga, which was so badly installed, when I had it properly looked at, it was actually quite dangerous (not to mention costing £700 a month to run – thankfully something Blake & Bull fixed for me and it's now far more efficient, cheaper to run and much more controllable, while retaining the classic look). This room has got the same wobbly laminate flooring as the living room, huge gaps where the cupboards should have been properly scribed and, all in all, it just needs a thoroughly good going over.

There's nothing fundamentally wrong with the cabinetry though. It's not the beautiful, handmade, solid wood cabinetry like upstairs, but is in perfectly serviceable condition and it would feel wrong from an environmental perspective to scrap it when, with a bit of love, I can (I hope) make it beautiful. I'll probably paint it and certainly fit it properly. I'll remove and sell the existing handles and put on something a little softer and more in keeping, and add some cornice and detailing to help it blend into its environment a little bit.

This room has got a great view out into the garden from the sink and, in the section of the garden it looks out to, I will eventually create a Georgian-inspired kitchen and cut flower garden, so guests will be able to wander out on an evening and cut some fresh herbs for their supper (assuming I one day learn how to grow herbs). The kitchen windows face west – the only ones in the house that do – which floods the space with light on a summer's evening.

There's currently a little banquette seating area for a small dining table, but, again, it doesn't really feel like it's up to scratch so will be coming out and replaced with something a little more in keeping.

The Remaining Spaces

Leading off from the kitchen there are two doors. Again, I believe these would likely have been on the external wall of the house, in the semi-circular bay window, but now are two doorways both leading through into what I believe is the Victorian extension. One goes through into what I think would have served as a pantry or creamery, or similar, as there are some old, thick slate worktops that would have been used for keeping food cool in the days before refrigeration. A quirky little space, with a couple of windows looking out to the garden, this has an old flagstone floor which is beautiful, but, having been laid directly on earth (as most floors of this age were), it does let moisture permeate through. It's something they were designed to do, and helps stop any form of rising damp being forced out and up the walls, but only works if we also then live as we did back then, with huge open fires taking any warm, moist air from inside and sending it up the chimney. In this age of sealing everything up tightly to make it more thermally efficient and replacing fires with central heating, the moisture in the air has nowhere to escape.

I think I'll turn this space into a quirky dining space, just off the kitchen with views outside. There's just enough room for a small table for intimate dining, and I think the rustic feel might even be a bit romantic once there are a few candles lit in there. An estate agent would likely call it 'atmospheric'.

The other door leads to a small utility space and then through that to another bathroom, done previously but very poorly. It's largely irrelevant anyway given it's currently leaking as the roof of this whole 'roof terrace' space needs redoing at some point, once funds allow. Again, it'll be redone to something more in keeping with the feel and period of this space.

I think there are likely eighteen months of work to be done down here to make it really lovely, but I'm very excited about the possibilities and can't wait to eventually open it up to share with people in some way.

FURNITURE

I'm asked quite a lot where I find all the furniture for Admirals. Obviously, moving in with naught but my clothes and a bed meant I was starting from scratch here and, well, with thirty rooms, there's definitely plenty needed. It'll be a very long, ongoing process filling the place, but one I'm very much looking forward to indeed, taking my time to find the perfect pieces.

You can probably tell from my pictures that I'm a fan of old, brown furniture – especially pieces from the Georgian and Victorian eras. This came about for lots of reasons really. Firstly, there's the way it looks, which I think takes some beating. With beautiful materials, proper craftsmanship, elegant proportions and design, combined with a good dose of patina and character, I think they add hugely to a space, regardless of the age or style of your home. Even if I were to own a modern, new-build apartment, I'd still use old pieces of furniture to bring in warmth and interest.

Another reason I love them is, well, because they are ridiculously cheap. The various chests of drawers and bureaus here were all between £40 and £100, the Victorian mirrored wardrobe in the yellow bathroom £60 and even the grand French armoire in the pink bathroom, still with its old, foxed mirrors intact, was £250, so when you're working on a budget, but still want something lovely and beautifully made, second-hand is a no-brainer (though I'm pleased – sort of, I would be fully pleased if I didn't have lots more to buy! – that the prices are now going up). These old pieces were out of favour in terms of trends for a while with the rise of minimalism and flat-pack everything, but now people are wising up to them and it's pushing up the prices.

Thankfully, people are also starting to think about the environmental impact of what they buy. There's still a long way to go, but just as people

are realising that 'fast fashion' – with clothing designed and made to a point that it's disposable after only a few wears – probably isn't a great way to clothe yourself from the perspective of the environment and are instead looking at both fewer, higher quality pieces that will last, as well as reusing/buying second-hand, the same is true for homewares. Anyone who's tried to move house with a flat-pack wardrobe will know that these pieces do not take kindly to that sort of wear and tear, using materials that don't last and that are usually full of fairly harmful things. Conversely, something that's already lasted 200 years is likely to keep going a good while longer and makes far more sense to me.

Of course, it doesn't make sense to buy everything antique. I'm not really very Georgian in height or stature and, as I've mentioned, often find their upholstered furniture just too small and not comfortable. This is absolutely fine for an accent chair in a bedroom or bathroom, but not ideal for settling down to a movie marathon on a rare, lazy Sunday afternoon. Obviously, fabric wears far more quickly than solid oak, and repairing or recovering something isn't cheap (and rightly so – having attempted to reupholster a simple chair, the work and man hours involved are huge). If you do go down that route, though, you will end up with something beautiful, completely bespoke and likely to last a very long time indeed. It's definitely worth having a go at upholstery if you've got something relatively simple, though. It's hugely satisfying and, if you take your time and think methodically, not as tricky as you might think (though a second pair of hands is very useful for most things versus trying to do it on your own). By upholstery, I mean things that don't require sewing, such as a footstool or headboard perhaps. The first piece of upholstery I ever tried was the dark green velvet supersized

number in the 'Room of Doom' (see page 166).

Older bedframes have similar issues around size, often being non-standard or, when they are, they tend to be a standard UK double, which, in my opinion, isn't ideal for two normal-sized adults to share comfortably for more than a few nights. Of course, in smaller rooms, it might be the only option. A random fact for you: the UK's standard double is the smallest 'standard' double bed in all of Europe and gives only 2 feet and 3 inches (69 centimetres) per occupant – that's less than we give a baby in a cot. A king, being 6 inches (15 centimetres) wider and, just as importantly, 3

inches (7.6 centimetres) longer, is far more comfortable, but if you have the space, a super king, with an additional foot (30 centimetres) of width over a king, feels very luxurious indeed for two. While you're unlikely to find one of these as a genuine antique, a newer, but still second-hand bed (but definitely not mattress!) is a great opportunity if you want something for much, much less than its original purchase cost. Again, if you're buying something of great quality, it'll last nearly indefinitely and, if you get it in the right style – a brass bedstead or classic sleigh bed, for example – it's timeless and beyond trends or

fashions. It can also be updated simply with the right bedding (and I've yet to see a bed that doesn't look brilliant with classic white linen, though it can be jolly hard to photograph well).

In terms of where I find my pieces, for lots of it, Facebook Marketplace has proven really useful, but there are a few caveats. Firstly, it seems to have become a hotbed of scoundrels and ne'er-do-wells looking to get one over on you, so please have your wits about you – their schemes are easily spotted and avoided, and you're generally pretty safe with furniture as you're more than likely going to view it and collect in person. Secondly, while it's possible to secure proper bargains when it comes to furniture, usually as people are keen to get rid of a bulky item for whatever reason and have no means of disposal short of breaking it apart for firewood, so you're doing them a favour, this only works if you can collect it – ideally offering to be there ASAP as you also need to be fast. The good stuff, when priced well, doesn't hang about, so you do need to be browsing quite frequently (the algorithm will quickly work out what you like, and usefully serve you up relevant items). Thirdly, when you spot something, don't try haggling (a difficult thing for a Yorkshireman to say). Offer them the full price and to be there as soon as is convenient for them – this is how bargains are had. Indeed, if you look hard enough, there's plenty of large, brown furniture offered for free if you can collect it.

Beyond that, another brilliant tool is The Saleroom, an online auction platform that essentially links hundreds of auction houses across the UK into one, searchable platform. This has been really useful when I've needed to search for specific pieces – the dresser base behind the sofa in the living room, for example, which I needed in quite specific dimensions. It allows you to search all the upcoming auction catalogues in one place which would otherwise take forever. Prices can vary, but, generally, for most stuff that isn't super fancy, it remains really affordable (just make sure you are aware of all the fees, and so on, on top of the hammer price). I was also able to have items couriered. eBay can be good too, but can be expensive now, I've found. Obviously, auction shops are lovely places to visit, but I just don't currently have the time to spend hours searching and wandering round. Most of my shopping is done at midnight when I'm done for the day and am lying in bed, or in snippets with a coffee when I need a breather from the graft – though I've rather romantic notions of one day having enough time to convert a van. (I once converted an old builder's panel van into a camper, long before it became trendy with the van-lifer types whom I'm often very envious of, complete with wood burner and Welsh dresser and absolutely loved it – my first 'project' if you will.) I would drive around the brocantes of France finding perfect pieces and trinkets … maybe one day!

Mirrors are another brilliant thing to buy second-hand as I just don't think modern mirrors sparkle like the old ones. Even the absolutely enormous, arched top one above the living room fireplace, which is nearly as tall as me and outrageously heavy – with its original mirror glass – was only £100 (and a bit of a pig to collect as it was bigger than my trusty little people carrier). Art too can be found for not much at all, often already in beautiful frames. The lady peeking out of the window and the demure-looking woman in the ornate black frame, both large oil paintings, were both £50 via Facebook Marketplace.

Other things to watch for include woodworm, though this is easily treated and not necessarily a deal-breaker, assuming the piece is solid (and most old pieces will have some evidence of woodworm). Damaged veneer, while repairable, isn't straightforward to repair if you're looking for perfection. Fortunately, I'm not, so happily have many pieces with bits and pieces missing (and be careful if you're planning to sand and refinish anything veneered – it's very easy with a powerful sander to quickly go through the top layer and ruin it). I always like to give things a good, gentle clean when I get them – vacuuming any dust, removing any old drawer liners, and so on, and then giving everything a good feed and polish, either with beeswax or a hard wax oil to get it looking its best and smelling grand.

I also wouldn't worry too much about getting things to 'match' either, in terms of period, wood type or tone. Indeed, the idea of a 'set' isn't my cup of tea at all (though I am partial to symmetry when it comes to bedside cabinets, but Admirals is a very symmetrical sort of house). In mixing and matching a little, you create a relaxing atmosphere that is not too stuffy and feels welcoming. It's worth remembering that most original occupants in these old houses would have come with a mish-mash of furniture just like most of us, and would have added to their collection over time to suit.

The STAIRWAYS & CONNECTING SPACES

The main stairs are actually quite dark, steep and narrow, without much in the way of natural light. They are going to need absolutely loads of work and clever lighting one day to make them as nice as they can be. The servants' stairs are, sadly, a real mess. Having suffered lots of damage from water ingress, they've also been butchered quite a bit in the past to allow for pipework and services up and down the height of the house. The top, where the stairs would have led to the third floor, was blocked off many years ago to create another room up there, and then a toilet was added as a sort of 'butler's toilet' literally on the staircase. It's all very strange! The landings themselves are very simple, as you can see from the floorplans – a strip off the stairs leading to the rooms.

The Staircases

This is where things get a little stranger. I've no evidence in the form of plans or similar, but I don't believe the main staircase, while very old, to be original. There's evidence of doorways (once I'd stripped wallpaper and so on) that, if still there, would open halfway on to a staircase. I think it's reasonable with a house of this size, for this period, that it would, once upon a time, have had a much grander central staircase. I believe that, when the house was split, the original servants' staircase would be what is now the main staircase for the third of the building that is a separate dwelling as it is of a size and style that reflects this. In losing its original servants' staircase to the separate house, it seems to me that two new staircases were added – one a grander spiral staircase and one a much simpler hidden staircase that would have been for the staff. When doing so, I believe the strange curved sections behind that now house toilets on the first and second floors were also added.

In an ideal world, I would love to remove the 'new' servants' staircase in its entirety, other than the flight to the lower ground floor. It serves no purpose, isn't architecturally interesting or nice, is in a terrible condition, cuts across windows that could otherwise be used to bring light into the house and isn't original to the house anyway. However, I think it's unlikely that I'd get listed building consent to make changes, though if I did, I could simply remove the staircase and turn the space that it currently takes up into rooms on each

floor that would be more useful and would respect the original windows and similar – but it's a long way before I'll have the time and energy to work out whether that's something worth pursuing. If the servants' stairs remain, then I'll likely shelve them out and turn them into quirky storage. A bizarre five-storey library if you will!

There's a feature on the main stairs that's quite unusual, and one that I've yet to fully get to the bottom of, despite asking the good folk of Instagram. A second bannister has been added on the tightest part of the stairs, leading from the ground to the first floor. It looks a little awkward, and certainly is lacking the pared-back elegance found in the rest of the house. One of the explanations, that might make sense, is that ladies' hooped skirts were popular when the change was likely to have been made. On the tightest part, in order for them to be able to reach the bannister, the secondary one, a little less near the edge where the stairs get narrower, would have been easier for them to reach. It feels somewhat far-fetched, but is so far the most logical explanation that there is (if anyone out there has a better idea, please do let me know).

There's a huge amount to restore in the staircases and landings, and it will be a lot of work. This will be the very last part of the house I'll be working on as, if I were to do it any earlier, it would simply get ruined as I go from space to space.

MY FOLKS

I wanted to add a wee section here about my folks – and more than just a thank you. As you can probably see from some of the photos here and from hearing a little about my upbringing, they are a huge source of inspiration to me, and have always set an incredible example (even if I mightn't have always liked it at the time) of what hard work and determination achieve.

Most of these pictures are of their last home (as well as some of them lending a hand here) – a chapel conversion that they bought already converted, albeit quite badly, so it needed a huge amount of work. They added a small extension and completely reconfigured it inside and out, with the garden in particular having had an enormous makeover. This was to be their 'final' renovation, and their eleventh in total, but three years after I moved down, they decided to sell up and make the journey to Plymouth to be closer to me (my sister has done the same thing so we're all down here now).

It was a bit of a wrench leaving the chapel behind – they'd done a stunning job, and had very much made it their own and it suited them beautifully. Countless hours had been spent on it, with them doing pretty much everything themselves. But, thankfully for me, they felt they had one more move in them and have bought the most incredible Edwardian lump that, while not in quite the state Admirals was, with seven bedrooms and nearly 5,000 square feet (465 square metres), it's not for the faint-hearted. It's got exquisite bones and I know they'll do a remarkable job – and they've very sweetly asked me to help too. It's certainly wonderful having them so close and I'll be eternally grateful for the support they've always shown me.

They're even responsible for the name of my Instagram account. My pa has a rather excellent collection of tools, one of which being a beautiful old Estwing hammer that he's had seemingly forever – so much so that he's had to remake the stacked leather handle himself. Well, they bought me one as a gift when I bought my first home and it remains a treasured possession with lots of memories attached to it, and felt like a fitting name for my page.

The
GARDEN

Now, it's fair to say this bit fills me somewhat with horror. As you'll have seen, my folks are brilliant gardeners, but, alas, so far, it doesn't appear that I've inherited their green fingers. When looking for a place to buy, I'd never wanted something with a large garden – so long as there's space to have a few friends over for a BBQ, a spot for me to sit out with a glass of something cold and a little privacy and quiet, then that's more than enough for me. Beyond that, it's just an awful lot of maintenance. But, the old girl came with what I think is about two-thirds of an acre (around 2,700 square metres) of what would once have been rather formal Georgian walled gardens – eek!

An Unknown Treasure Trove

AND LOTS TO LEARN!

Arranged across a couple of levels to account for the slope down to the bottom, when I took the house on, the garden was a mass of brambles, weeds and mess – the brambles were so wild and thick in places that there was a whole greenhouse hidden beneath them that I didn't know about before getting the keys.

The garden is full of mature trees, including a huge tulip tree and a massive yew, as well as reportedly being home to the oldest mulberry tree in the south-west of England, sitting right in the centre of the bottom lawn, looking very, very old indeed having been struck by lightning on more than one occasion, and now being chocked up and supported with various iron bars, lumps of oak and straps. Quite how much longer it's got in it I'm not sure, but it still crops incredibly heavily and is perfect for making mulberry gin.

I've yet to make any formal plans for the garden – perhaps that'll be book number two! – but I do know that I'm going to have to get learning as I really want it to live up to the house again one day. Due to it having been a naval house, there aren't the outbuildings or land one would usually associate with a plot of this size. The hospital grounds had stabling for the officers' horses and anything needed to maintain the house and grounds would likely have been kept communally by the staff who looked after such things in various buildings and workshops throughout the site.

On that basis, I will, eventually, need to build myself some kind of workshop and tool storage out there. Currently, my tools are strewn throughout the house, in the various rooms still to be renovated, but obviously, as I finish more and more rooms, this is becoming tighter and tighter, and maintaining a house of this size and age requires a lot of 'stuff'.

REPORTEDLY THE OLDEST MULBERRY
TREE IN THE SOUTH WEST OF ENGLAND

I think I'll have to get some help with the design. Knowing nothing about plants, I'm a bit clueless as to what to plant where, and will no doubt get things horribly wrong if I don't seek out some advice. I'll obviously do the graft myself though – it's going to be fairly backbreaking as it will require some pretty serious landscaping to properly reinstate the levels and paths that have been slowly allowed to disappear over time. The boundary wall is likely going to need some serious attention at some point too, as well as rotten gates and fences replacing. The roof terrace's railings, a later addition, are rusted and bent beyond saving (and weren't terribly high-quality in the first instance, looking very out of place next to the beautiful original cast-iron Georgian railings). All the old railings front and rear need the paint removing and repairs making before being repainted. Luckily, as the house has the lower ground (and it's quite a fall down there), the railings at the front weren't sacrificed during the Second World War to help with material shortages for the war effort, as they were across most of the country where removing them didn't represent a safety hazard, and give a great reference point for any replacement railings that are required.

The courtyard at the back, underneath and around the roof terrace, an area I believe once would have been busy with the working staff in the house, again is in a terrible state. Concrete has been poured very badly over the original stone, without proper levels on it to facilitate drainage, which has, in turn, led to rot where water has been pooling in doorways leading to cupboards, the boiler room and a decidedly grim outside WC.

The courtyard at the back, underneath and around the roof terrace, an area I believe once would have been busy with the working staff in the house, again is in a terrible state.

So long as I've a glass of something cold and suitably adult in my hand, and a deckchair to sit in, I can be perfectly happy outside.

I've rather grand plans for this little space – an outdoor shower and bathroom of sorts, perfect for cleaning off when I've been working in the garden or been for a swim down at Devil's Point and am too grubby to come into the main house; rustic, but with a little luxury. I also think it's crying out for a simple outdoor kitchen of sorts down there that will hopefully one day have a smoker and pizza oven, as well as reinstating a huge Belfast sink I found in one of the rooms. I'd also like to add a general covered working area where I can make a bit more mess than I might dare in the kitchen if I want to make enough pizza to feed an army or similar, for example!

Still, this all feels a very long way off. I deliberately chose to start on the house. My budget isn't big enough to even do that all in one go, let alone anything chunky on the garden.

I know there are lots of people who say to start with the garden as it takes time to bed in and grow, but, of course, the second you start, you then need to keep on top of and maintain a garden, every single year – which would mean even slower progress on the house as I try to stop it turning back into a jungle as things grow like billy-o here in Devon. I also didn't (and, well, still don't) have the budget to do everything required and am going at the pace I can, doing things as my budget will allow and, when moving in, it's fair to say a working toilet took precedence over rose bushes!

A house obviously requires maintenance, decoration doesn't last forever and things can break or get damaged, but it's a fairly finite thing – once it's done, broadly speaking, it's done. That is very much not the case with the garden and, despite working all the hours physically I'm able, there's no way I'd be able to spare the man hours needed to keep on top of any work done – I've even given up trying to mow the lawn with my little push-along mower (it's good for the bees ... that's what I tell myself, and anyone else who asks). One day, though, it will all be glorious – honest.

INSTAGRAM

It would feel remiss of me not to talk about Instagram and the role it's played in my renovations (and, indeed, my life) – after all, without it, there would be no book to speak of!

It all started back in December 2016 with my first post – still up if you can be bothered to scroll back a while. It's just a picture of me standing by the back of my last home with a Christmas tree, so nothing to get terribly excited about.

I didn't really know much about Instagram then. I wasn't a huge user of social media generally, nor especially adept at picture-taking or anything like that, but I'd had a look and there seemed to be a rather nice community of renovating house-y types on there, sharing experiences and ideas, so I decided to join the fray. I was a bit embarrassed by it all if I'm honest, and didn't tell my friends and family I was doing it, but I was proud of the renovating I'd done at that point and, given it can be a bit lonely and hard at times, feeling some camaraderie with others going through the same thing was jolly nice indeed. I'm not sure when 'influencers' became a reality (a hideous term, but one that seems to have stuck; I just wish it didn't have some of the negative connotations associated with it), but there didn't seem to be any such thing back then, and there was certainly no motivation of that type for joining on my part. I didn't expect anyone to really follow along in any great capacity, but it felt like a nice thing to do all the same, as well as a good place to document the final few rooms of that home.

Well, all that changed a bit when the lovely Kate Watson-Smyth, of previously-mentioned @mad_about_the_house fame, somehow stumbled across my little account, complete I think with its 200 or so followers at that point, and asked if she could feature it on her blog of the same name. I was ridiculously excited and really, truly honoured.

Kate's blog had been one of the key drivers for me to start learning about design and the ideas and principles around it (it's still brilliant, as are her books and they're highly recommended if you're looking to learn or for inspiration). I don't come from a world where interior design felt like it was something for me, but Kate put it in a way that seemed accessible, logical and practical, which appealed massively.

With such exciting news, I couldn't really keep it a secret from anyone anymore. Featuring on Kate's blog introduced some new people to my little page and I think in a week I'd hit a lofty 500 followers! I couldn't quite believe it, but everyone was very kind indeed and it felt lovely, after so much hard work, that people felt like I was doing a good job.

From there, I kept plugging away, posting what I could about the house, and the account continued to grow a little bit. I made some friends, and even went to a big party at the home of lovely Katie @comedowntothewoods with about a hundred home Instagram types – other than a few husbands and partners, I was, hilariously, the only chap there with an actual Instagram account. It was so much fun and, again, everyone was lovely, kind and supportive.

Well, at that point, I think there were maybe 10,000 people following along. It was still quite a small community in terms of the number of people actually sharing their home online, but it was with a slightly heavy heart that, given I was selling up and likely to be without a home of my own for a while, I let the account go dormant. I didn't want to just post personal 'stuff'… it was, and likely always will be, primarily focused around renovating and my home – albeit with a smattering of life sprinkled over the top – and I never wanted to feel like I was posting for the sake of it, so I just left it there.

Fast forward eighteen months or so and, with the old house sold and having exchanged on Admirals, I thought it would be a good time to see if there was anyone still out there who remembered me and might be interested in me having taken on the old girl. So I posted a full-frontal of the new lump. There was the loveliest response – people seemed genuinely excited for me, which was so charming. More than that, though, in the time I was gone, Instagram seemed to have had a bit of a surge in users and interest in home accounts, and lots of the lovely people I'd become friends with previously had done brilliantly, growing their accounts to what seemed, at the time, ridiculously huge numbers. So many were kind enough to share my new home and some, like Katie, have gone on to become firm, real-life friends with many a boozy evening spent together chuckling away.

Since then, I've been sharing pretty much everything I've been doing here, and it's been remarkable how interested (and patient!) people have been, with me doing what seem to me at the time the most mundane things (months spent paint-stripping and sanding definitely doesn't feel like terribly engaging 'content'!). I do pride myself on sharing the 'reality' of it all, though, and in fairly real time so people get a proper sense of what it takes to renovate a lump like this.

It's been really wonderful sharing what I do, albeit also a huge amount of work … trying to juggle a full-time job, actually renovating, taking content to share and then posting and keeping up with people's questions and comments – which is ultimately my favourite bit of social media – regularly saw me working 100+-hour weeks, week in, week out. But, I loved it.

It is so heart-warming to see people's excitement for Admirals and the work I am doing here. More than that, it is incredible to get feedback from followers telling me that, having seen me

tackle something, it has given them the confidence to give it a go in their own homes. It really does feel like the most wonderfully wholesome thing.

Well, fast forward a bit more and we all found ourselves in a lockdown. Obviously, this was a devastating time for countless people with work, businesses and lives hugely affected. But it did give us all more time at home … myself included. I found myself furloughed from my job (I worked for a baker's at the time that made cakes for the wholesale market, selling into tea rooms, cafes, attractions, and so on, that were all closed). With this extra time – and still receiving a percentage of my salary – it meant I was able to really crack on and make some headway with the house, and spend a bit more time talking about it on Instagram too.

It was a bit of a perfect storm I think. All of a sudden, we were confined to our homes far more than we ever have been and our relationship with them in that period changed significantly too, becoming much, much more important to us. Previously, where we might have been happy with something slightly minimalist – our lives so busy going out, working, living, and so on that we prioritised easy to clean and look after over interesting and beautiful – a lot now yearned for comfort, colour and pattern. Making a home our own became more important than it ever has been.

On top of that, Instagram became a place where far more of us 'hung out'. Again, unable to do much more, it was escapism, companionship, a space to be creative, to learn and be inspired, so our screen time inevitably went up, with more eyeballs than ever before on 'content', and, inevitably, masses of that content was focused around the home given there wasn't a lot more we could do. As more people shared their homes, I believe our expectations around what our homes looked like increased. We also weren't spending any money we might have in the pub, at restaurants, on holidays or on fancy frocks and expensive shoes – there wasn't much point when we couldn't go much further than the dining room (if you were lucky enough to have one … I certainly didn't at that point, but I'm very grateful I had plenty of space inside and out, and a gazillion things to keep me busy here through the lockdowns; I know it wasn't like that for a lot of people) – so, all of a sudden, there was this huge interest in home improvement.

Beyond that, it was also a period when interest in period properties – especially those from a similar period to Admirals – seemed to be going up. I'm speculating, but I think it's partly a result of the reasons above, but also because of some popular cultural references – *Bridgerton*, *Downton Abbey* and *The Crown* on the telly definitely felt like they had an impact.

So, my little page continued to grow and people remained hugely supportive, and, as it grew, some companies got in touch keen to work with me to help showcase and highlight their wares in my restoration. That all seemed to go better than I ever could have hoped. All of a sudden, I found myself having to register my business, find an accountant, work out how to use their software and prepare VAT returns. Again, this was hugely exciting, but lots of work. By the time it came to go back to work, it seemed like the business had established itself enough to take the leap and give it a go – now or never. At the time of writing at least, it seems to be going OK – and, more than that, while I've really enjoyed some of the jobs I've had and the businesses I've worked for, and loved the people I've met along the way, they've never really felt like a calling.

With Instagram, and sharing the journey of restoring Admirals House, I seem to have stumbled upon something I am truly passionate and excited about. I (usually – we all have our off days!) get up in the morning, excited about the day ahead. On low days, it feels like I've got thousands of people cheering me on. I share ideas I might not be sure on and it's been hugely helpful – the hive mind well and truly working a treat. It is so satisfying knowing people have been inspired to give things a go themselves, and also holds me accountable on days when I might not feel like doing much – motivating me – which is no small thing with a project this size. Overall, it's something I am just hugely grateful for.

Instagram has also allowed me to work with some brands I could only have otherwise dreamed of being able to use here at Admirals, and the work is enormously satisfying. It is definitely work though – and a lot of it. It's been a little quieter while I've been book writing, of course, and settling my folks and sister into life down in Devon and their new homes, but at any other time, the Instagramming (by which I mean anything to do with running the business, whether that's actually time spent on Instagram, taking and editing photos and videos, talking to brands, negotiating contracts, doing the business-y stuff like accounts and book-keeping, and chasing payment when people ignore your invoice – which is more frequent than you'd think) is 40+ hours a week. Of course, in order to have any content (and get the house done one day!), I need to renovate too, and I try to do maybe 30+ hours a week on that, so it's a bit like having two jobs …

It takes WAY longer than you'd think to run an Instagram page around renovating, particularly now Instagram has moved towards more video content, which is much more labour-intensive than tidying up and styling a space for a photograph. At the time of writing – and something I will continue to do as long as I physically can – I respond to every comment and message I get. Currently that's averaging over 1,000 every time I post, and the last time I counted, when more active and posting stories almost daily,

3–5,000 direct messages a week, so if you have a question or need advice or similar and you send me a message, it's very likely I'll get back to you – and important to me to be able to do so.

I could probably write a whole book about Instagram itself and my approach to it, but one thing I would say is that, even though it's lots bigger than it used to be, it's still the loveliest community of supportive, like-minded people, so if you're renovating and thinking about starting an account, I heartily recommend it. However, don't go into it thinking you might one day become the next Kardashian or similar – it's not something that's easily within your control – but as a space to share ideas, learn, vent and generally just feel a connection to people who might be going through a similar thing to you, it is wonderful, well, 99.9 per cent of the time. Of course, like anything else interweb-related, it comes with exposure to people who seem to forget their manners occasionally when hidden behind a phone screen or laptop, but thankfully that is a very rare exception to the rule that most people in the homes and interiors world are jolly nice indeed.

It's also worth bearing in mind that Instagram, and all kinds of social media, changes rapidly, and you've no control over it … we're currently in the era of viral videos, with accounts seemingly able to go from zero to a huge following overnight thanks to one catchy clip. It's the nature of the beast and all you can really do is roll with it, and do the best you can.

All I would say is stay consistent and true to yourself. If you do this, you'll find your people, they'll find you and hopefully you'll have some fun along the way without having to resort to the latest dancing fad or, perish the thought, use a 'trending' song.

Lots of wonderful things have happened off the back of @manwithahammer that I think are worth sharing. Obviously, this very book would never have happened without it, and meeting Albert and his family (see page 24) would have been very unlikely too. The friends I've made through it and the business and calling it's given me are something I shall be forever grateful for, and there's been lots more besides. My bedroom graced the pages of the New York Times, for example, which blows my mind, and I even found myself on the BBC talking about lead poisoning … but, as much as those big things are amazing, it's the connections you make with people that are the most special – and it really does feel like I've got my own personal support network.

As an example of this, about four months into working on Admirals, I did a very silly thing when absolutely exhausted at the end of a long weekend working on the house, involving lighting a fire when it was far too damp to do so. I'll spare you the details, but I managed to set myself on fire and genuinely had to 'stop, drop and roll' which broadly worked, though petrol had soaked into my sock, which acted as a wick as the flames went up my leg. Adrenaline kept me going for a bit and, when everything was under control, the searing pain kicked in. I whacked my leg in cold water for as long as I could stand while downing the half bottle of wine in the fridge. I stuck a load of antiseptic cream on it, wrapped it in cling film and considered it good to go, but not before taking a few snaps for Insta – good content and all that jazz!

Well, I wasn't quite expecting that much of a response beyond 'what an eejit', least of all from lots of lovely medical professionals, including one from the actual burns unit here in Plymouth who told me, in no uncertain terms, to go to A&E as it might have needed serious treatment. All's well that ends well, and it's all healed a treat, but I thought it was just a rather lovely example of the sense of community that can surround you with Insta. It's something I am grateful for – for so many reasons.

A Final Note

With nearly five years under my belt as the custodian of Admirals, at the time of writing, I had (very naively) thought I might be nearly finished with the renovations. Oh, how we can all laugh at that poor, optimistic soul! As it stands, there are about fifteen further rooms inside to finish, plus all the stairs and landings (and there are so many stairs), a lot of work to the fabric of the building too with all the windows needing fairly significant attention, alongside the outbuildings and courtyard, as well as the garden to get my teeth into and learn about. The restoration of Admirals is rapidly becoming my life's work and I think there's comfortably another eight years' worth of solid graft (and certainly a lifetime's worth of maintenance) to go.

But, ultimately, that's OK. There was never really a time limit to how long it needed to take. It was never taken on for profit or to sell – just to make my home the best I can – and, most importantly, I am thoroughly happy in my work, most of the time. While that remains the case, well, it can take as long as it takes really. That's not to say it's not busy and exhausting, and I think now I've reached the point where the old girl is, in the main, a comfortable place to be, I'd like to be able to find a slightly better work–life balance between running my business, renovating the house and actually living, as it's fair to say the latter has been very much compromised to get to this point.

For as long as there's interest in it, I'll continue share what I do, in my own, erm, 'special' way, in the hope it might inspire a few people to give things a go themselves and create homes they love, while saving and protecting some of the incredible architecture and built heritage we collectively have, both here in Blighty and across the world. I will always be happy to share any of my (limited) advice or words of encouragement over on @manwithahammer for as long as my thumbs work.

Sources

THE GROUND FLOOR

The entrance hall
Flooring: Broadleaf Timber, Admirals Oak
Lighting: pendant light, Pure White Lines; sconces, Lumière du Jour; shades, Samarkand Designs
Paint: woodwork, Fenwick & Tilbrook, Sheringham Beach exterior eggshell; ceiling, Fenwick & Tilbrook, Dandelion
Table: Laskasas, Ann dining table
Wallpaper: Zardi & Zardi, Chinoiserie panoramic in chalk white

The kitchen
Aga: Blake & Bull
Blinds and window seat cushions: Warner House, Amoli Indigo
Cabinets: made bespoke by Heaven & Stubbs
Flooring: Broadleaf Timber, Admirals Oak
Fridge: Liebherr
Lighting: all from Lumière du Jour
Paint: Fenwick & Tilbrook, Before Dawn, Little Donkey and Sheringham Beach; woodwork, Fenwick & Tilbrook, Sheringham Beach exterior eggshell; ceiling, Fenwick & Tilbrook, Dandelion
Radiators: Cast Iron Radiator Centre
Taps: all Perrin & Rowe in polished brass
Wallpaper: Warner House, Lilou in blush
Wood burner: Stovax, Air 1
Worktops and splashback: Algarve Granite, Carrara marble

The living room
Built-in bespoke alcove cabinet: Heaven & Stubbs
Curtains: Warner House, Mughal Trail Cinnabar
Flooring: Broadleaf Timber, Admirals Oak
Hearth: Algarve Granite, Carrara marble
Lighting: Pooky Lighting
Paint: as per entrance hall
Radiators: Cast Iron Radiator Centre
Rug: Crucial Trading, Sisool
Suzani: Loom Designs

Television: Samsung Frame
Upholstered furniture: all Warner House
Wallpaper: Warner House, Lilou in charcoal
Wood burner: Dovre, Vintage 50
Everything else is second-hand

The smallest room in the house
Paint: Fenwick & Tilbrook, Moss exterior eggshell
Panelling: The English Panelling Company
Tiles: Tile Giant
Toilet: Burlington Bathrooms
Wallpaper: Warner House, Jaipur Ivory

THE FIRST FLOOR

The main bedroom
Art: Tom Glendenning and Diane Hill
Bed: And So To Bed
Carpet: Crucial Trading, Small Boucle Sisal
Chair: Warner House
Curtains: Warner House, Horsham Navy (velvet)
Lighting: bedside lamps, Samarkand Designs; table lamps, Pooky Lighting and Lumière du Jour
Paint: Fenwick & Tilbrook, Burnham Overy and Nelson's Hideout
Pendant: Pure White Lines
Radiators: Cast Iron Radiator Centre
Tapestry: Zardi & Zardi
Everything else is second-hand or antique

The pink bathroom
Art: Diane Hill Designs
Bathroom fittings: Burlington Bathrooms (excluding the bath, which was second-hand)
Chair: upholstered in fabric from Harlequin by Diane Hill Designs
Curtain and blinds: Laura Ashley
Lighting: main pendant, Pure White Lines; toilet pendant and wall lights, Original BTC

Paint: Fenwick & Tilbrook, Woodland Jay and Sea Henge
Radiator: Cast Iron Radiator Centre
Tiles: Mandarin Stone

The party room
Cushions: Anna Hayman Designs
Mirrors: Dominic Schuster
Ottoman: fabric by Anna Hayman Designs
Paint: Fenwick & Tilbrook, Drunken Sailor
Rugs: Axminster and The London Persian Rug Company
Table lamps: Pooky Lighting
Wallpaper: Anna Hayman Designs, Party Room

THE SECOND FLOOR

The 'room of doom'
Blanket: Maund Interiors
Carpet: Crucial Trading
Fabric and blinds: Warner House
Lighting: Pooky Lighting
Paint: Fenwick & Tilbrook, Mudlark, Highland Peat and Dandelion
Radiator: Cast Iron Radiator Centre
Wallpaper: Warner House, Palampore Archive
Wardrobes: Heaven & Stubbs

Bedroom four
Art: Musee Home
Blanket: Maud Interiors
Chairs: Barker and Stonehouse, Drew Pritchard range
Curtains and fabric: Warner House
Fireplace tiles: Original Style
Lighting: Pooky Lighting
Paint: Fenwick & Tilbrook, Little Donkey and Dandelion
Wallpaper: Warner House, Fleurs Orientales Cameo

The yellow 'bathroom'
Art: Musee Home

Basin: London Basin Company
Bath: second-hand
Paintwork: Fenwick & Tilbrook, Holkham, Damselfly and Dandelion
Panelling: The English Panelling Company
Taps: C. P. Hart
Wall lights: Original BTC
Wallpaper: Zoffany, Cochin in blue

Bedroom seven
Art: Musee Home
Carpet: Crucial Trading
Curtains: Warner House
Fireplace tiles: Douglas Watson Studio
Lighting: Pooky Lighting
Old plates: Rock the Heirloom
Paint: Fenwick & Tilbrook, Greylag Goose
Wallpaper: Warner House, Summerby Wedgwood

The Chinese bathroom
Art: Musee Home
Bathroom bits: Burlington Bathrooms
Flooring: Broadleaf Timber, Aged Oak Parquet
Lighting: Pooky Lighting
Otomi: Loom Designs
Paint: Fenwick & Tilbrook, Greylag Goose
Panelling: The English Panelling Company
Tiles: Original Style
Wallpaper: Warner House, Les Pecheurs China Blue

THE LOWER GROUND FLOOR

The Bedroom
Bed and furniture: Laura Ashley
Carpet: Kersaint Cobb
Lighting: Next
Paint: Autentico, Earth Stone and Chalk White
Rug: Next
Wallpaper: Next

I Would Like to Thank...

My oldest pals, The Baxes, Chris and Rose, who I admire hugely and want to thank not only for a lifetime of friendship and inspiration, but for having such a hand in shaping me into the chap I am today (for good and occasionally ill!).

The wonderful Moodys, Mark and Holly, for whom I'm hugely grateful to now have round the corner ... for feeding and watering me so well, keeping me sane through the dust and having endless patience with my nonsense!

The team at Hodder & Stoughton who have turned this very much non-author into someone who has managed to write a book with a huge amount of their help, support and expertise. From Lauren at the beginning having the belief this might actually work and Liv's endless patience when I might not have quite been running to time, to Julia for the mammoth task of editing my waffle into something legible and Nikki for turning my very scrappy sketches and ideas into something truly beautiful.

The brands, companies, agencies and people I've had the pleasure to meet and work with throughout my time as custodian of Admirals House: there are so many it's impossible to name you all personally, but I am hugely grateful and, I'm sure, should she be able to talk, the old girl would be too.

Last, but very much not least, Katalin, for being the most wonderful distraction I could ever have imagined.

First published in Great Britain in 2024 by Catalyst
An imprint of Hodder & Stoughton
An Hachette UK company

2

A CIP catalogue record for this title is available from the British Library

Hardback ISBN 978 1 399 70869 2
eBook ISBN 978 1 399 70870 8

Publisher: Lauren Whelan
Senior Project Editors: Liv Nightingall and Charlotte Macdonald
Editor: Julia Kellaway
Art Direction and Design: Nikki Dupin, Studio Nic&Lou
Photography: Andrew Burton
Illustrations: Andrew Cadey at andrewillustrates.com
Senior Production Controllers: Matt Everrett and Rachel Southey

Historical information on the site of Admirals House has been taken from: *The History of the Royal Naval Hospital*, Plymouth by P. D. G. Pugh, OBE, Surgeon Captain, Royal Navy (reprinted from the Journal of the Royal Naval Medical Service, vol. 58, pp. 78–94; 207–26, 1972) and *Up the Creek* by Graham Evans (G. V. Evans, 1994).

Colour origination by Altaimage London
Printed and bound in Germany by Mohn Media

Catalyst
Hodder & Stoughton Ltd
Carmelite House
50 Victoria Embankment
London
EC4Y 0DZ

www.hodder.co.uk

This book is written for entertainment purposes only and should not be taken as an instruction manual. Any DIY or other building project you undertake is at your own risk and you should always seek advice/assistance from qualified tradespeople.